MACHIAVELLIAN MANAGEMENT

A Chief Executive's Guide

Malcolm Coxall

Edited by Guy Caswell

I0102245

"The Truth shall set you free"

Cornelio Books

Published by M.Coxall - Cornelio Books
Copyright © 1985, 2012, 2013 Malcolm Coxall
First Published in Spain 2012
ISBN: 978-84-940853-1-4

Contents

Preface

Machiavelli, the myth

For centuries his name has been demonised: a synonym for evil, a master manipulator of the masses and creator of a kind of amoral realism whereby the ends justify the means. His book, "The Prince", has been described as a guidebook for tyrants.

Yet others praise him as the founder of modern politics in the Christian world, the man who really invented the phrase - *get real* - whilst some view his work as the stirrings of the concept of human rights.

What was he really like, this personable figure that spent his days drinking and playing cards in the pub with the locals whilst his evenings were dedicated to writing one of the most important books in Western literature? A man who wrote the most popular comedy of his time and yet wrote a book still fiercely debated today.

What did he discover that makes him so relevant today? In our 21st century era of spin doctors, image builders and 'damage control' mass media experts, could it be that Machiavelli, 500 years ago, perceived some truths of man's nature that have lessons for us today?

Machiavelli, his world

Machiavelli grew up in a Europe that was fast changing. The Renaissance was revolutionary; man was starting to see the world in a new way. Copernicus displaced the world as the centre of the universe with the sun; Leonardo Da Vinci dissected cadavers to understand the workings of the body.

Observation, not old doctrines or theory, was the new approach. Awareness that man was the master of his own fate was taking root.

And in the chaos of a 15th century Italy, divided into countless city-states and principalities with constant internecine conflict and wars, lived Machiavelli, a loyal civil servant, with a passion for politics and a longing for a united Italy.

"The Prince", the longest job application in history

In 1494 Florence expelled the Medici family who had ruled for 60 years and restored the republic. Machiavelli, aged only 29, was appointed to a diplomatic council and for 13 years he undertook various diplomatic missions abroad. However the return of the Medici in 1512 saw him thrown out of office, accused of conspiracy, imprisoned and tortured.

Finally released, he was banned from entering Florence city. To a man who lived and breathed politics this was a cruel sentence, spending his days supervising his family's farm and estate, he started to write "The Discourses", focusing on the desirable attributes of a republic.

But Machiavelli yearned to return to politics so he suddenly abandoned "The Discourses" and furiously wrote "The Prince", a manual on how to obtain and remain in power, in 3 months. He presented it to the Medici family, urging them to become the nation founder of Italy.

Machiavelli's relevance today

In his diplomatic missions abroad Machiavelli met many princes and leaders gaining and losing power in the fractious and constantly changing political landscape. He witnessed the 'functional' use of violence by the Borgias, he learned what new leaders had to do to assert themselves. In this jungle and anarchy of shifting alliances and disloyalty, he analyzed and dissected the methods and psychology necessary for survival of the leaders and the city-state.

The Song Remains the Same.

Five centuries have rolled by, but the human condition hasn't changed, only the surroundings.

Power broking, stand-offs, bluffs and promises, rhetoric and hard talk, nothing has altered in the human psyche since Machiavelli penned his masterpiece, whether it be in the Italian courts or the boardrooms of London.

An essential understanding of "The Prince" will reveal to the rulers and ruled the hard facts of human politics, both then and now.

An apology to female chief executives: Ladies, I would like to offer my sincerest apologies for constantly referring to the executive as a male in this book.

I assure you it is simply for convenience, to save space and maintain readability. Faced with a choice, we decided to stick to Machiavelli's original choice of gender.

I am fully aware of the tremendous and rising number of female managers and executives in our world today and the vital role they play. No slight or disrespect is intended in the use of the masculine gender in this modernisation.

If the English language gave me an opportunity I would gladly neuter our executive but that could possibly undermine his or her authority and prestige, and we can't have that, can we?

---oOo---

1. The Executive Prince: An open letter to all chief executives

It's always a pleasure to pay tribute to those whom we respect in the political or business arena. What better way to do that than with my small contribution to our knowledge of good executive management practice, based on my understanding of the deeds of great and successful executives of the past and my extensive analysis of the methods of contemporary politics in business and commerce?

I have summarized my conclusions here and I now offer this little book to chief executives everywhere. I know this is not the definitive work on the subject, but it is the sum total of many years of experience, observation and consideration. It is a simple and straightforward document, focusing on a serious subject.

I hope that it will not be considered presumptuous (given that the author has never been a chief executive) to give advice to those elevated to the heights of corporate management. But I speak as one who has always been an unquestioning and loyal adviser to senior executives for many years.

It is often easier, I believe, from this humble position as an adviser, to define how a chief executive ought to behave, and to understand how to manage the affairs of his employees and company.

So, ladies and gentlemen, take this offering in the spirit in which it is intended, read it and consider it carefully.

I hope you will discover here my earnest hope that you will ultimately get what you undoubtedly deserve.

Adapted from Niccolo Machiavelli's letter of dedication to the Magnificent Lorenzo de' Medici - "The Prince".

---o0o---

2. Companies and how to acquire them

Types of Companies

Virtually all organisations, in which a hierarchical management exists, fall into one of the following categories. All are discussed in this text:

- Independent private companies
- Large Public companies (national-multinational)
- Subsidiaries of large public companies
- Semi-state companies
- Civil service departments
- Cooperatives

Independent companies and their subsidiaries have private managements and a group of private shareholders. Public companies and their subsidiaries have managements notionally responsible to public shareholders, but within certain limits they are independent. Semi-state bodies/companies are ultimately responsible to government, as is the civil service. Cooperatives are responsible to their members.

Types of executive control

All these organisations are controlled by "chief executives", of one kind or another, though they do not always hold this title or enjoy exactly the same powers in all types of organisation. All "companies" may be long established or new ventures. They may employ their own acquired or inherited capital, or that invested by others.

Executive control of any company may be achieved in one of five ways:

- Inheritance
- Personal ability
- Opportunism
- Election
- Crime.

---o0o---

3. Independent Family companies - The personal touch

Preamble

Gaining control of a family company isn't usually a matter for much discussion or conflict because the decision as to who becomes chief executive is normally preordained. For example the eldest son of the family or some other method of inheritance is usually how control is passed from generation to generation.

The risks and defences of the family company

The crux is how to hold onto your company. In this dangerous world of corporate take-overs, buy-outs, dawn raiders and aggressive acquisitions, it can be hard to maintain control of a small family company. In this world, a chief executive is judged by his ability to fend off external predators.

However, there are some lines of defence in old established companies against these kinds of external risks. And the most powerful of these defences is to maintain the old, nostalgic, feudal respect and support of the middle management and workforce towards the family and the traditional alliances with long standing customers. The company's "ancient retainers" are the most potent defenders of the family company. They are capable of extraordinary sacrifices to maintain their status quo - for example, being talked into working for little or no pay in appalling conditions during difficult economic times simply to defend the old company.

Advantages of old family companies

Examples abound in the "old industries" of family companies which pay their employees a poor wage for long hours in archaic working conditions with draconian company rules. And yet, incredibly, these organisations still have many employees, at all levels, who have served their company and its owner family for decades and who wouldn't dream of questioning their management ability or their rights as employees.

Thus is the depth of sentimentality between employee and employer in these old dynastic companies. This extraordinary phenomenon gives a chief executive an excellent opportunity to prosper personally and to protect his position as CEO. He is surrounded by employees who are personally, emotionally involved with the ethos of the company and they will sacrifice a great deal to defend it and him at almost any cost to themselves.

But to be successful, a chief executive of this kind of company needs to apply some basic rules if he wants to resist unwanted change: Firstly, he must not neglect the traditional institutions of the company, however trivial they may seem, especially those founded by his ancestors and most cherished by his employees. He must, of course, be aware of the threat of unwanted acquisition, adapt his policies and make plans in advance to deal with these and other commercial threats. But of all the defensive policies he implements, maintaining the status quo is the most powerful tool the CEO has in a family business. By upholding the status quo, he also recruits and co-opts every employee as a defender of the company.

Staying in power in the family business

By appealing to the innate "conservative" attitude of his workforce, a good CEO can be assured of complete internal support, if he plays his cards right by keeping the old retainers on his side. If a chief executive in a family company is hard-working and intelligent, and readily supports the traditions of the company, he will not be readily deposed by anybody.

In addition, if a conservative CEO is successfully deposed from his family company by a takeover or some other mechanism, then his successor is going have a hard time during the transition. The existing management and workforce will be critical towards any new executive, antagonism and the absence of any personal fidelity will be obstacles facing the new CEO. This can be very much to the advantage of the deposed chief executive, should he wish to re-establish himself.

Regaining Power in the family business

In these circumstances, the natural reaction of any displaced chief executive is to start another company, usually along the same lines as the old one. He will use whatever resources he has to do this.

If he does this immediately after he has left his old position (whilst still close to his ex-employees' hearts), it should not be too difficult for the deposed executive to actually recover control of most of the key constituents of the old company, i.e. markets, contacts, key personnel, product-knowledge, designs etc.

If he has looked after his loyal staff and shareholders in his old company, an ousted CEO will be in a very good position to exploit its resources by taking advantage of the fidelity of his ex-employees and customers. If he has treated them well they will readily provide him with the means to recover his position again, because their allegiance is personal, and not simply economic.

The CEO's Priorities in the family business

So the main priority of the CEO of a family firm, or other long established independent companies, is to look after the old company's workforce, to neither rock the boat nor implement any dramatic changes, unless there is absolutely no alternative. Upsetting the old retainers might endanger a chief executive's position, whereas doing nothing poses few risks.

If these faithful employees are content with the feeling of continuity and security provided by the traditional family management, why should it not continue as always? Provided that the chief executive does nothing to lose their respect, they will assume that it is his or his family's natural right to run the company and manage them.

People will tolerate poor pay, bad working conditions and inequality simply to maintain the continuity and stability of a relationship which makes them feel safe and comfortable, even if it is a semi-feudal relationship like a family company.

---oOo---

4. New companies and newly acquired subsidiaries

Differences between new companies and family businesses

New companies and recently acquired subsidiaries are a very different proposition to an old family company. Starting and maintaining control of a new company, or acquiring and holding onto a new subsidiary, is far harder than simply retaining the status quo of a long established family business. The two situations require a radically different set of skills from the CEO.

A company acquired

If a company acquires a new subsidiary or takes over a new start-up enterprise, then the process of consolidation into a parent corporation will be a lengthy and traumatic one. There will be a lot of uncertainty and misplaced expectations in the air.

But, after the initial trauma of the take-over, life will probably go on as usual without too much dissention in the new company/subsidiary, provided that the more "sacred" of the existing internal institutions and practices of the acquisition are left untouched for a while.

Suppliers, customers, incumbent management and the workforce will initially accept their position because they will also hope and expect to gain personal advantage under the new management.

But these expectations will be mostly unrealistic and will soon be dashed as the new management begins to purge and reshape the newly acquired company. The disappointment and resentment this causes will aggravate matters considerably, leading inevitably to hostility towards the new management. Prudent, and yet decisive management, timed to perfection, is essential in this situation.

In this event, a new chief executive may be obliged to injure or sacrifice those who may initially have supported him, to consolidate his position and impose his authority on the new company.

This is particularly true of start-up companies acquired by venture capitalists where the original entrepreneurs and their entourage may need to be removed quite quickly, in order to allow for the development of the core operation of the company. Good start-up people rarely make good managers, but few entrepreneurs recognise this about themselves and this is sure to be a source of resentment after a company is acquired.

When a company is taken over, it may or may not be engaged in the same business as its new investor. When the parent and subsidiary are in a similar business, it is somewhat easier to establish and maintain effective control because there is some sense of understanding of the common business which both companies share.

It is also the case that a takeover is easier when a subsidiary is not really used to being totally independent, or has previously had extensive business dealings with the new owner. In these cases, the transition may well be less "bloody".

Establishing control of an acquired company

To establish effective control, a new chief executive must remember two things:

-    All the retainers of the previous management may have to be removed from the company, regardless of whether they are managers, supervisors, workers or members and friends of the previous owner's family. In fact, this purging of an acquired company is nearly always a necessity. (There are some exceptions which we will discuss later on).

-    In the early days of a takeover, a chief executive must appear to show respect for the existing infrastructure and working practices of his new company and not interfere with them in any way. In this way he can minimize the alienation felt by the company's personnel and consequently neutralize any hostility before it occurs and develops into disruption. In this way, most of the employees, management and customers can be smoothly assimilated into the parent company.

Maintaining Control of an acquired company

When an acquisition is of a company in a totally different type of business, there are greater difficulties. Maintaining control requires a tremendous effort on behalf of the new chief executive. The most effective course of action here is for the chief executive to micro-manage his new company in person on a day-to-day basis until the take-over is complete. He can then get to know his managers and employees and learn the intricacies of the business at first hand. This is probably the only way of securing the company. It would be a big mistake to just take over a company and just expect it to continue as if nothing had happened, because naturally everyone will take advantage of the change in ownership to promote their own interests.

For example, when Anflex Ltd.[3.1], a large paint manufacturer, purchased a controlling interest in Brindley Building Supplies, a hardware distributor; the new subsidiary's turnover took a dramatic downturn. This was because during the transition period there was a certain amount of confusion with sales promotions being suspended and no launch of any new promotions.

The company's competitors naturally saw the change of management as an opportunity to move into the distributor's territory. The old management of Brindley was reluctant to take any action although they were fully aware of what was going on. Fortunately, the chief executive of Anflex noticed this sudden change in the fortunes of his subsidiary, and immediately took over the daily management of Brindley in person, along with a small team of his own best marketing and sales managers. He quickly analysed the situation, and with the help of some incumbent managers, reasserted Brindley's market position.

Being on the spot, a chief executive can naturally detect disaffection amongst employees and customers, and indeed other commercial problems in their early stages, and consequently take immediate remedial action. In contrast, an absent chief executive will only recognize a problem when it is too serious to manage easily. As all doctors know, a disease in its early stages is difficult to diagnose but easy to cure, later it is simple to diagnose but may be impossible to cure.

In addition, the policy of "showing a presence" deters both the management and workforce from taking advantage of a chief executive's absence in other ways. A workforce is also happier in this situation because it feels that it is taken more seriously, and therefore merits the chief executive's presence. If present in person, a chief executive is unlikely to lose control of the company and the company is more likely to prosper.

Organising your supporters in a new company

An important extension of this principle is to place senior managers from the parent company into key positions in the organisation of a new subsidiary. This is an effective way of keeping a finger on the pulse of the new company. The only persons injured by this action are those deposed by the new managers. These deposed managers need to be very carefully and decisively removed, with no delay, so that they cannot do any damage to the new CEO. This may well involve paying for their cooperation or other more coercive means of getting their cooperation in leaving.

Thus, the surviving managers are given a taste of the strength of resolve of the new chief executive, and will be doubly cautious in their behaviour.

In many respects, the careful alteration of the management structure of a new company/subsidiary can be a very good strategy indeed, but it does require a great deal of care in implementing these changes, as I will explain here.

Dealing with new employees in an acquired company

In general, a chief executive has only two ways to treat his employees and fellow managers: either he can be generous towards them and hope that they will cooperate with him, or he can force them into compliance. Astute use of this combination of generosity and compulsion is the sign of a talented, effective and successful CEO.

But how are these two contradictory management policies perceived by the average employee or manager? Whilst employees may seek revenge against a chief executive for some small grievance if the opportunity arises, they will think twice about defying a CEO whom they know will retaliate decisively and resolutely, possibly resulting in their instant dismissal or removal.

Grievances in a newly acquired company

An example of a grievance could be the installation of a number of new managers from the parent company. The consequent upset and offence felt by the other managers and employees, whilst not affecting their jobs, may be pernicious and pervasive.

If hostility persists, a safer policy would be to fire and replace the entire management team[3.2]. A good CEO must not be frightened of doing just this, and he should make sure that all the incumbents know that he is capable of doing this if necessary.

A chief executive must also quickly take steps to protect his new company against the predatory behaviour of the company's competitors who may seek to capitalize on the disaffection of employees, management and customers which might take place before, during and immediately after a take-over.

In our previous example, Brindley Ltd, the distribution company above, experienced a short period without close executive management. During this brief period, many of its suppliers and customers saw an opportunity to profit due to the absence of management and temporary confusion within the company. They attempted all kinds of ploys, such as unilaterally demanding extra credit, insisting on extra discounts, free delivery conditions etc. They hoped that the new chief executive could be persuaded that these arrangements had been agreed "before his time", and that he must honour them.

The management vacuum created by the take-over process presents an excellent opportunity for competitors, employees and other predators to promote their own interests at the expense of the company and the new chief executive.

Boldness of action by new CEOs

In summary, any new chief executive faced with the mentioned situations, must avoid timidity or squeamishness. He must remember that the desire to acquire is a common human trait; people naturally seek opportunities to profit from the confusion of change. Therefore a good CEO must be both firm and decisive, factors that will win the praise of his employees and fellow managers. He will gain little from being needlessly generous or lenient and his reputation will suffer if he is perceived to be weak or a failure as an executive.

---o0o---

5. Maintaining control

Preamble

Holding onto the helm of a company is the next big priority for a chief executive. And here it's interesting to observe how the different management styles and personalities of the CEOs influence their company's response to arduous times.

Causes and effects of corporate disruption

For example, why is there an upsurge in dissent and disruption in some companies following a sudden change in management, such as the death or resignation of a chief executive, whilst in other companies, the management team just continue to run the company competently and quietly until the arrival of a successor?

The reason is that all companies are fundamentally managed in one of two ways:

- By an autocratic chief executive upon whom everyone is dependent, his management team is merely to assist him (the micro-management control freak).

- By a chief executive supported by managers. Crucially, the credentials, influence and respectability of these managers are seen in the eyes of subordinate employees to be more important collectively than those of the chief executive.

Management styles and handling disruption

The autocratic chief executive has great personal authority - everyone else is considered just an assistant to the omni-powerful boss. His management team have little real authority and gain little respect and loyalty from the workers. In this case, when the boss goes, chaos tends to break out.

Management of disruption: The small private company

Small private companies are often very autocratically micro-managed because they rely mostly upon the driving ability of their chief executive, from whom initiatives usually stem. Whenever there is a change in executive management, there is always trauma and strong resistance to the new management. However, once a new chief executive is fully accepted, allegiance to the old management is easily and totally transferred to him.

In contrast, the second type of chief executive is secondary to his own management team. The managers control their own departments as if they were departmental chief executives with a lot of autonomy and authority. Their subordinates' first loyalty is to their manager and not necessarily to the chief executive. This type of company continues virtually undisturbed, despite the comings and goings of chief executives.

Management of disruption: The civil service

The civil service and military are excellent examples of this second type of management structure. Senior civil servants and their sub-ordinates direct their ministry or department pretty much regardless of which government minister or political party is currently heading the ministry. They are little disturbed by changes at the top.

It is rare for any civil service to change rapidly or fundamentally. When it does change, it morphs very slowly, more by a process of evolution than as a result of a deliberate ministerial policy. Along with the armed forces, the civil service represents a most highly developed and rigid form of hierarchical yet devolved management. It is based on the inter-dependent and resilient structures of feudal government with its kings, princes, barons, squires, landlords, tenants and peasants. No-one is indispensable, yet all are, to some extent, mutually dependent on each other.

In a government department, every local unit has a supervisor to which lower grades report. Several units are managed by a district manager. Districts are organised into counties, provinces etc., all with their own hierarchical manager. Special purpose autonomous units have their own managers. Almost no-one reports directly to a minister.

A local unit supervisor considers that he or she is answerable only to their regional managers, who, along with other regional managers, are controlled by a permanent under-secretary who is responsible for the specific function of his department. His department is one of many within a Ministry. Such complete devolution divests a Minister of any contact with, or allegiance from grades lower than under-secretary. This makes for a very resilient and stable hierarchy which tolerates instability at the top with little discomfort.

Management Styles: Types of organisational structures: autocratic and devolved

Continuing our comparison of the autocratic and devolved organisational structures, a good rule of thumb is that whilst it is very difficult to take over an autocratically run company, it is very easy to maintain it. And vice versa: It is relatively easy to become chief executive of an organisation run by its middle management, but it's difficult to establish and maintain real control of it.

It is hard to gain control of a autocratically run company as an outsider because there is little or no chance of being invited in or helped into power by the existing management team. They are completely loyal to, dependent upon and "under the thumb" of the autocratic chief executive.

But once the old autocratic regime is replaced, the old chief executive removed and his inner circle placated or dismissed, the new in-coming chief executive is in a very secure position.

So whilst he got little help in gaining power from the old retainers of the company before his takeover, a predatory new CEO will have little to fear from them afterwards.

In contrast, getting control of companies run by middle management is a great deal more straightforward with none of the complications of loyalty, fear etc.

It is a fairly simple "political" matter to create enough discontent amongst the management, workers and shareholders to gain control of a company like this. There are always those who are dissatisfied and desire change, and these people can be instrumental in opening up the company to such a predator.

However, having taken the reins of power, the chief executive of this type of company will run into countless difficulties in maintaining his control for he commands neither respect nor fear from managers or workforce. Companies with a dominant, autonomous middle management do not take kindly to a new chief executive attempting to impose control over them.

And he will be threatened, not only by those whom he has deposed, but also by those to whom he has made fanciful promises and who assisted him to power.

It is therefore very likely that the new CEO will have to remove many supporters as well as any detractors. It won't be enough just to eliminate those in the management team who supported the old order. He may well have to purge both friend and foe alike to hold onto his position.

In comparison, employees in companies run by an autocratic management are more laissez faire about their chief executive's behaviour when he is established because they are accustomed to non-consultative change.

In conclusion, a chief executive planning control of a new company, should remember that his degree of success will depend not only on his ability, but also on the type of company he is acquiring.

---oOo---

6. Managing new acquisitions accustomed to independence

Preamble

Some companies are accustomed to being independent and they don't adapt easily to being taken over or becoming a subsidiary of some larger company. In such cases the new CEO can expect considerable resentment and opposition towards him. He should be ready with an appropriate strategy to deal with such eventualities.

Strategies for gaining control of independent companies

In the case of newly acquired companies, there are four basic strategies which can be used to establish and maintain control:

- Scorched-Earth: The Company's assets are stripped and anything of no value to the CEO is dumped. The essential and most valuable components from the company such as capital, fixed assets, key-personnel, products, patents, technology and customers are removed for use in another enterprise which the CEO already controls.

- Palace Coup: The Company is purged by immediately removing all those who oppose the new chief executive and replacing them with trusted retainers from outside.

- Farming: The Company is kept intact but operations are micro-managed in person on a day-to-day basis. Factions opposing the CEO are brought round whilst employees dependence and loyalty to the new CEO is cultivated by making gradual changes in management.

- Proconsul: The Company is left intact but a popular and efficient member of the existing management is appointed to look after the day-to-day operations. The CEO simply accepts involvement at arm's length and takes the profits, whilst making sure that everyone knows where the ultimate authority lies.

Maintaining control of an independent company

Ideally a company is managed by its own personnel, as described in the fourth of our options above. However, it is absolutely essential that the semi autonomous management team is made fully aware that they cannot exist without the goodwill of the chief executive. They shouldn't get any presumptive ideas about regaining their independence. It is important that the onus is upon them to make a definite effort to maintain both their position and the authority of the CEO. This requires a subtle combination of ruthlessness and sensitivity from the new CEO.

Hostile Takeovers and management purges

Let's look at the case of Harbury Plc., a large London publishing house. As part of its policy of acquiring provincial media companies, Harbury took control of "The Gravesbury Examiner".

The Examiner was a well-established newspaper in the north of the country. It had good sales and a loyal readership. But the deal immediately ran into trouble because Harbury was simply incapable of imposing its management's will on the new subsidiary.

The opposing political interests of the two companies created a vicious conflict with the management of the newspaper being openly antagonistic to their new owners.

For Harbury, this rapidly became a major problem. It couldn't realistically remove all the opposition without also losing the newspaper's best personnel, its readership and its public image. In fact, if it purged the newspaper's management it would effectively destroy the asset for which it had just paid £25million!

The management of Harbury quickly recognised that they could be faced with an embarrassing and costly financial disaster if they didn't act quickly and pragmatically.

First they approached the talented and popular deputy editor of the newspaper with a deal. They guaranteed him editorial autonomy and a handsome shareholding in the company if he cooperated in a planned "re-organisation". He readily agreed and was proud that he had won a good deal for the editorial integrity of his paper.

The next morning the managing editor of the newspaper and his immediate staff were fired by Harbury and asked to leave the offices at once. It happened so quickly that no one, apart from those being dismissed, actually knew anything about it.

Harbury moved quickly to consolidate their position. They made popular promotions amongst some of the existing personnel, paying them big "fidelity" bonuses. The new deal of editorial independence was sold to the public and staff alike as a sign of the great independent tradition of the newspaper. Within weeks, the status quo had returned and the new owner of The Gravesbury Examiner was largely forgotten. Those few who remained antagonistic to the holding company found very little support amongst their fellows and gradually drifted away.

Hostile Takeovers and asset stripping

There is also the instance where the chief executive has no intention of keeping the operation in business and simply wishes to use the assets or useful personnel for some other purpose. In such a case, he may simply wish to strip the assets from his new acquisition. This strategy is sometimes referred to as "Creative Destruction" because it uses creative management and accounting in order to bring about the deliberate destruction of an asset.

Such was the case of Gentex Corp., a huge international business software company. It developed an interest in Tiny Ideas Ltd., a small "vertical market" software house, which had developed some very innovative manufacturing management software. It had a small dedicated user base but was growing quite rapidly. Because of its small capital base but fast growth, Tiny Ideas Ltd was in constant need of refinancing and flexible credit.

It took only a short time for Gentex Corporation to find an opportunity to offer Tiny Ideas some serious capital in return for a small shareholding. Within two years Tiny Ideas was a wholly owned subsidiary of Gentex.

Gentex took over the management of Tiny Ideas and ran the company, albeit half-heartedly, for six months. During this time, the products and workforce of Tiny were gradually incorporated into Gentex. New orders coming into Tiny were side-tracked to the parent company and little by little Tiny Ideas ceased to exist as a commercial force.

Eventually, under the pretext that Tiny Ideas Ltd had almost no business, the chief executive of Gentex officially wound up the company. The "creative destruction" was complete.

Some of the best design and supervisory staff of Tiny Ideas were offered alternative employment in Gentex. Its offices were closed or incorporated into Gentex holdings.

This strategy lost nothing for Gentex, the parent company. Indeed, it achieved a satisfactory overall improvement in market and sales for a one-off capital investment. In addition, by absorbing its subsidiary, Gentex eliminated any risk of losing control of its acquisition later. So it simultaneously gained total control of the acquired company's most essential and valuable assets: its products, technology and people, whilst also eliminating any competitive downside from a small but irritating competitor.

Despite the apparent harshness of this takeover, Gentex Holdings management was not without some scruples. In fact, it was considered by its employees to be a very liberal company.

Originally Gentex had considered keeping Tiny Ideas as just a subsidiary. The plan had been to extend the management of Gentex to their new subsidiary. However, after consideration, the Gentex management felt that there was too great a risk of disruption to its own markets by a separate, but similar company like Tiny Ideas, a company with a completely different management ethos to the giant Gentex Corporation. In the end, it was considered more prudent to simply strip Tiny Ideas of its assets, removing the old company completely. [5.1].

There is no doubt that the most certain method of getting and keeping control of a new company is simply to strip it of its assets and dump whatever remains as quickly as possible.

Managing Hostility

The last sentence above is particularly pertinent for those taking control of a really independent minded company. If the incoming CEO decides not to dismantle it, he can expect trouble at a later stage when the company runs into hard times of some kind. In times of misfortune, the old management and personnel will blame the decisions of their new owner for all ills. After all, they have no loyalty to the owner, so why should they support him? The antagonists in the company will always cite the "good old days" of their "independence" in complaints about their current troubles. Absolutely every problem will be laid at the door of the new chief executive - regardless of his actual performance and capability. However great the ability of the chief executive, however generous he is, he must be aware of these risks.

Because of this danger, a new CEO must be capable of understanding, infiltrating and eliminating hostile elements in his new company. If he does not do this he will never eliminate the "good old days" phenomenon, the inherent conservatism, and the many old allegiances. At the first opportunity the incumbents will attempt to re-establish their influence and exert authority in an attempt to return to their past independence.

Independent companies are often very attractive acquisitions because they are frequently highly innovative with uniquely valuable skills and products. But they are also much more conservative and distrustful of external interference or change in their ownership than subsidiaries. Thus, there is a much greater likelihood of employee disloyalty. The memory of independence and their hurt corporate pride is ever present and this must be carefully managed by the new chief executive and his team.

On the other hand, independence is not such a major issue for subsidiaries. Accustomed to being controlled by a faceless parent company, they simply transfer whatever allegiance they have to the new (anonymous) owners. Both acquisition and management run more smoothly than with independent companies.

---o0o---

7. Acquiring a company by skill and personal resource

Skill versus Opportunism (I)

A person may become a chief executive of a company through various methods, but in a nutshell the CEO either uses his skills and resources to build or buy his own company, or he is a clever opportunist, taking over a company when a suitable opportunity arises.

The Skilful Manager

Let's consider the example of the chief executive who achieves his position entirely independently, just based on his own capital and skills. He achieves this using his own personal financial resources and management ability, rather than through any example of opportunism. This situation has its own strengths and weaknesses. A chief executive in this position must adopt completely different strategies to one who has gained his position opportunistically.

Generally, the chief executive (the new CEO) in completely new companies will encounter only a small number and type of problem. Because he is skilled he will manage to deal with these management problems without much difficulty. A chief executive who relies upon management ability (rather than "luck") is in a much stronger position than his opportunistic counterpart. This is especially true when it comes to consolidating the gains of a new enterprise. This is an important point for all chief executives and it's worth illustrating in more detail.

I am going to cite a few fairly grand examples to illustrate the differences between the opportunist and the skilled CEO. I make no apology for this; after all, these individuals have done more to alter the modern world (generally for the good) than any politician. Whether we actually "like" these individuals (Gates, Jobs, and Wozniak etc) or their companies or not is actually irrelevant. Their exponential rise, incredible personal successes, and enormous impact on the world is undeniable. There are lessons we can learn from such people, i.e. CEOs who gained their success, wealth and power by their own skills and ability.

There are plenty of examples of those who have achieved their high corporate station by means of their personal ability. The obvious candidates are the Hi-tech gurus of the 1970's who powered their way out of their parents' garages to forge the technology revolution which continues to this day. Apple, Microsoft. These brilliant young people (Gates, Jobs, and Wozniak etc.) were exceptionally innovative, motivated and adaptive. They possessed a natural energy and entrepreneurial spirit to rise to the top with only the very smallest opportunity. Without their exceptional ability they would never have succeeded in establishing and maintaining control of their substantial global corporations. For them, skill was more powerful than opportunity. These individuals literally "created" their own opportunities out of almost nothing but their own exceptional abilities.

The role of opportunity

This isn't to say that these people did not have the advantage of any opportunity. That would be inaccurate. They all had a good education and came from fairly stable middle class families. The times were economically quite good. But when we consider the degree of innovation in their work, their technical vision, ability and leadership, we can see that opportunism, in comparison, played almost no part in their success. Certainly they could not have consolidated their achievements had they not been so able and competent.

Different perceptions of risk and opportunity

An important factor in any discussion of management ability versus opportunism is the individual's perception and reaction to opportunity and risk.

An able chief executive is realistic about risk, but an opportunist is not - he sees only opportunity but little risk. An opportunist is lucky if he happens to make the right management decisions, at the right moment, but it is just luck - not ability. That is because the opportunist sees opportunities as completely positive and will generally miss or deliberately ignore risks. This is what sets these two personalities apart. An opportunist has a heightened awareness for a good opportunity, but few skills to help in consolidating his gains.

But it's not quite that black and white and we have to qualify these definitions somewhat. For example, an able chief executive who does not have an opportunistic streak in him, is as useless as an opportunist who has no real ability.

Skill versus Opportunism (II) - An ideal combination

An opportunist will not survive without acquiring some basic management ability and an able executive will not achieve his goals simply on the basis of being competent. He must have opportunities and the instincts to recognize them.

The ideal chief executive, therefore, is one who combines real skills with a nose for a good opportunity. He knows when to be adventurous or opportunistic, and when to rely on his managerial skills and be circumspect. He must be, in a word, flexible.

Becoming an opportunist

Often business opportunities (and opportunists) emerge from times of great difficulty and privation of some kind. Many (in fact most) large corporations started their lives as small private companies struggling to survive. It seems a natural part of their evolution to have suffered in their early years, from lack of recognition, shortage of finance, understaffing and overwork, etc., in order, ultimately, to graduate into becoming really big, profitable, efficient mega corporations[6.1].

Take for example, Hantronix Ltd, a specialist electronics manufacturer, founded in the garage of its owner, with an excellent idea but no money. The company spent some years being financially stunted, its staff underpaid and overworked, and not considered a serious rival by any of its competitors. This company however, was driven by a determined and ambitious managing director. When it finally did get a break and receive some proper funding from a private equity fund, the company blossomed. Because it still maintained a very prudent fiscal policy and great adaptability, the company emerged as a "lean and mean" competitor on the international market. If it had been well financed from the beginning, would it have been so successful?

At the same time, the development capital company which was opportunistic in taking a controlling interest in Hantronix Ltd., could not have made such a good investment without the opportunity to acquire such a mature and sound, (but cash starved) company.

So we see that very often successful opportunities and opportunists are born out of hardship. Someone's hardship is often the necessary precursor to someone else's opportunity. But whilst opportunists may acquire corporate power quite easily, they frequently hold onto it with great difficulty.

This is in contrast to CEOs with great ability who may struggle to gain control of their company, but once successful, are able to hold onto their power much more easily than the opportunist.

Skill versus Opportunism (III) - Managing Change

The real test of a capable executive lies in the successful management of change, for example, when a CEO attempts to implement organisation reforms, such as new reporting systems, work practices or alternative management styles.

Nothing is more difficult or dangerous for a chief executive than instigating big changes in an established company, especially when the alterations affect daily working practices or undermine job security or payment.

A newly installed chief executive will have many "hidden" enemies within the existing management team. When it comes to implementing changes, these employees will rarely support the CEO with his innovations. They will naturally mistrust anything which they have not previously experienced, and they will fear that they will lose their status after any big changes.

In this situation, whenever a possibility arises to attack or discredit the new chief executive, these old retainers will do so vigorously. The defence available to the CEO will be weak, simply because he will not yet be sufficiently established and this can create a very dangerous environment for our newcomer.

How the new CEO handles these challenges depends very much on whether he is basically a skilled manager or whether he simply relies on his opportunist instincts.

Skill versus Opportunism (IV) - Strategic thinking

There are some important differences in the reaction and behaviour of the two personalities:

An opportunist chief executive, lacking more subtle management skills, will not have taken time to reinforce his position in the company. He won't have bothered to make strategic alliances or work out all the little cliques in his management team, decide whom he can and cannot trust.

The more able chief executive, having gained his position, will have immediately and methodically attended to these matters and be prepared to take evasive and disciplinary action in a surgical and considered way against all opposition.

The opportunist will not have considered the possibility of these threats and will be taken completely by surprise. This is because his talents lie, not in management, but in the astute recognition of opportunities.

Consequently the opportunist chief executive will often fail to maintain any real changes he tries to make in his company, and he may ultimately lose his position entirely because of his failure to consolidate his gains, a failure stemming from the absence of any real ability[6.2].

The importance of financial independence

In addition, we also have to consider the value of independent financial resources to a chief executive. There are those who are financially self-sufficient, and there are those who depend upon others for their capital. The financially assured chief executive can overcome most problems by recourse to capital - his own capital, and consequently there isn't much risk of his being deposed or losing control of the company.

In general, a chief executive whose wealth, personal contacts and self-reliance are substantial will be successful regardless of the circumstances. This is because capital resources can always be used to exert persuasive pressure either on other shareholders or employees.

But a financially weak chief executive is at much greater risk. He can rely only on his ability or opportunistic instincts to persuade his shareholders to support him financially, and he must constantly justify his decisions to others. He is ultimately completely reliant on these individuals and they may not have the knowledge or understanding of a particular situation to make an informed decision. And so an economically weak CEO is more or less an "employee", rather than a leader, surrounded by shareholders and employees that resent his presence and any changes he attempts to implement. Certainly he will probably get verbal agreement from colleagues on any issue or plan but it will be a great deal harder to translate this into honest enthusiasm and support.

This, of course, isn't a satisfactory situation and this brand of chief executive is frequently seen changing jobs on a regular basis or starting his own company.

In conclusion, it is essential for the successful chief executive to arrange his personal financial affairs to give him the highest possible degree of independence. No-one operates well from a position of weakness and it must be made clear to everyone from the shop floor to the customer that in no circumstances is it possible to deflect the chief executive from his objectives with economic threats of any kind. They must realise that ultimately he doesn't need their support. In terms of independence, it is also helpful if a chief executive has only a limited amount of other business commitments, so that his hands are free to manage his company without distraction.

Achieving financial independence demands a tremendous initial effort on the part of an aspiring chief executive. This early period is a most difficult time. However, once independence is achieved, a chief executive will be universally respected. He is then in a confident position to remove any subordinates who are envious and disrespectful and to silence or neutralize shareholders who oppose him. Success is then almost assured.

---o0o---

8. Acquiring a company by opportunism

As mentioned, generally speaking, an opportunist gains his position with little effort but holds onto it with great difficulty. Before we study some examples of the opportunist in action, let's take a closer look at his personality.

What is opportunism?

The first thing to note is that opportunism is not just about being able to spot and exploit a good business opportunity when it emerges. It is a lot more complicated than that.

An effective opportunist must often exploit and use various factors such as nepotism, bribery, internal conflicts and ingratiation before he can "open up" and seize a good opportunity. Chances don't come "on a plate", they often have to be "created", and this is the "art" of the opportunist.

Negative aspects of opportunism

However the undoubted skills at setting up and seizing a good opportunity are little use for the opportunist in times of extremity or rapid change. This is because the opportunist relies entirely on the predictability of other people's behaviour. He assumes that there is goodwill towards this person or idea, antagonism towards that policy, that there are petty rivalries, allegiances and local political attitudes which, when taken together, allow other people in an organisation to be easily manipulated.

But this reliance on human behaviour rather than hard fundamental management skills and business realities, makes an organisation controlled opportunistically an intrinsically unreliable power base when the going gets tough.

So, an opportunistic chief executive in difficult times is often incapable of holding on to his position for very long unless he is also a particularly able person and that is a very rare combination.

Opportunism without good management rarely succeeds

The opportunist will not have consolidated his position with acts of good management, and therefore he will tend to fail at the first crisis. If the individual concerned happens to be a fast learner, it is possible he may be able to consolidate his position and in this case there is some chance of survival.

By way of illustration of these two types of CEO, it's interesting to refer to two examples: the first is the case of the opportunist with little ability and the second is an example of the able man with little opportunity.

Ingelton, Harbury & Associates, an advertising agency, was managed by a chief executive and six partners[7.1]. One of the junior partners was somewhat disgruntled. He felt that the fortunes of the company were not altogether healthy because of the incompetence of the CEO. In reality, the company was going through the normal seasonal downturn in activity. But the junior partner was very confident and ambitious. He firmly believed that he could do a better job than the chief executive despite the achievements of the CEO over the previous twenty years. It wasn't long before the junior partner started to make plans to take control of the company.

The junior partner was basically a technician and had little management training or experience. But he was responsible for the drafting office which was a fairly strategic role. In addition, he had established a friendly relationship with many of the company's younger clients and firmly believed that they would prefer to see him running the company rather than his more conservative, older managing director.

And so, following his plan to take control of the company, he began, more and more, to ingratiate himself with these clients. Simultaneously, he contrived to cause delays in project deliveries by means of all kinds of tricks such as requiring continuous design redrafts and manipulating conflict between the partners regarding the acceptability of a particular advertising campaign. These delays and apparent inefficiencies became quite noticeable after a short time and it wasn't long before clients began to complain about the delays, much to the delight of the junior partner. When a client complained, he would take great pleasure in blaming the plodding attitude of the old chief executive. Gradually more and more customers became dissatisfied with the company's performance, and accounts began to close.

The junior partner however continued to keep up contact with these disgruntled customers socially. He never failed to pour out to these clients his dissatisfaction with the performance of the old chief executive. Sometime he undertook free-lance work for the old clients. Needless to say, these projects were delivered "on the dot", just to demonstrate his own efficiency.

At the same time, within the company, the junior partner started to carefully manipulate his colleagues. He soon disaffected the other partners and the company's employees towards the CEO, with complaints of business being lost by the chief executive's poor planning and management. He took pains to remind everybody, whenever he could, of the impending threat of redundancy caused by their "inept CEO".

The penultimate stage of the partner's plan was completed when he mortgaged his house and raised a substantial personal loan, prepared for a buy-out and waited for his opportunity to come to fruition.

The opportunity came at last when the company suffered the loss of its largest contract. A high budget advertisement had been delayed in the art department and the client had missed a crucial product launch. The advertising contract was promptly cancelled.

In the absence of this large chunk of routine business, the company's situation suddenly looked extremely grim. Redundancies were unavoidable. An extraordinary meeting of the company's board was called, and a heated argument took place with accusations of mismanagement flying in all directions.

The junior partner saw his chance and played his "ace". He produced a chronology of lost clients from the previous eighteen months. The evidence was damning and it seemed clear to everyone that the chief executive was losing his grip and something had to be done urgently to save the company.

The crisis had crept up on everyone (apart from our opportunist junior partner). No-one had sufficient personal funds to put into the company to allow it to ride out the storm, except of course our junior partner who explained that he had inherited a sum of money and was willing to invest on certain conditions. Of course, the main condition was soon clear, he was to be appointed managing director and the old CEO was to take early retirement. The net worth of the organisation was now extremely low but he explained that he was willing to take the risk to save the company for the sake of the employees and other partners.

And thus it was that the chief executive's resignation was demanded and received and the ambitious junior partner was elected as chief executive.

All would have been well had this individual had any management ability or business sense, but alas he didn't! All he had was an ability to see and exploit weakness in others, manipulate his weaker colleagues and the company's clients, and this he had done very well indeed!

However the damage he had done to the company's business was not as easily reversible as he had expected. Many clients had taken their business elsewhere, and he had so badly sullied the company's reputation that potential clients were very wary of putting their trust (or their business) with the company.

Many key employees, fearing redundancy, had found a job elsewhere and were leaving at a steady rate, despite the new regime.

Within a few months, the new CEO, lacking both business experience and personality, found that he was unable to motivate either his employees or the other partners. The negative tide of the company's fortunes which he had created was unstoppable, and after a year the company was declared bankrupt, as was the hapless opportunistic chief executive.

So this was a case where an opportunist, bereft of management skills, fairly easily gained control of a company by some adroit manipulation, but was completely unable to run the company successfully - simply because he lacked any managerial ability.

Good management with few opportunities can survive

Now here is an example of a CEO who had tremendous ability but few opportunities:

Startronics Corp. was a small, U.S., specialist microchip manufacturer, controlled and managed by its president and six vice-presidents, one of whom was responsible for international marketing.

The president himself controlled domestic sales. The executive responsible for international marketing had little respect for the president's management ability, and rightly so in a sense.

As a manager, the president of Startronics was inept and weak. At heart he was a "techie" electronics engineer. His colleagues often commented that nothing else seemed to matter to him except new development projects. He also didn't take very seriously either international marketing or the people responsible for such non-technical activities.

When he did talk about sales, he seemed more interested in the saturated US market and his conversation would inevitably return to the subject of his latest product-design.

The young VP of international marketing was becoming increasingly frustrated by the attitude of the president and helplessly watched corporate competitors making inroads into Startronics global markets. Finally, he decided that, if the company was to prosper, the president would have to be removed from the management team. He therefore set out to oust the president and take control of the company himself.

After much wrangling and persuasion, the young VP secured a budget from the company and substantial grant assistance for the construction of two assembly plants and marketing divisions in Europe and Latin America.

He hired well-qualified and dedicated managers to assist him in their operation and appointed well-established and aggressive distributors to handle the company's products.

Within eighteen months the company's global sales had quadrupled. The level of production in Europe and Latin America soon exceeded that of the US facilities. The VP of International Marketing became VP of International Operations. He was then able to extend the company's non-US activities to include local component sourcing, quality assurance and some minor R&D. International sales continued to surge ahead whilst domestic US sales remained more or less static.

Soon, the VP's success was rewarded when he was also given responsibility for US sales. The president, still unaware of the looming threat, was grateful to be relieved of this irksome task, and continued to spend most of his time in the research department.

The VP of marketing had become highly respected amongst the other vice-presidents. Indeed he was well-liked by everyone in the corporation, and was seen as being primarily responsible for the company's new wealth and prestige. Simultaneously, the president was rapidly becoming irrelevant in the eyes of most of the company's management.

After two years, the young vice-president felt it was time to take his rightful place as CEO of the company. Thus began the final part of his strategy.

On the pretext of a quality assurance problem, the vice president suspended all product shipments. Turnover plummeted at once and within a few weeks the economic position of the company was looking quite alarming.

Secretly, the VP negotiated an option on some external equity. After four months of no production, the drains on the financial reserves of the company were catastrophic. The quality problem was no nearer to being solved, even with all the company's engineers working on it day and night.

A meeting of the board was called to discuss the crisis and the vice-president of marketing tendered his resignation on the grounds that the situation made his position untenable. He firmly laid the responsibility for the quality problems at the feet of the president and his design-team. On top of all their other problems, the loss of their talented VP of marketing was the last straw for the board of directors. They pleaded with him to stay and see the company through its troubles. He promised to consider it.

Next morning, having allowed the executives to "stew" over their predicament, the vice-president called another meeting, and explained that he had thought over his decision to resign. He offered to withdraw his resignation, conditional to being appointed president and sold a controlling amount of the company's stock.

The president, he suggested, should devote his time to what he undoubtedly did best, i.e. research and development. The other VPs readily supported him. The president, desperate to save his company and seeing the VP as its only salvation, stepped down and accepted a non-executive position in the company's research department.

The new president was aware that back orders were in jeopardy now and knew that he had to move quickly to consolidate his position. He called a meeting of his engineers and made some suggestions regarding the possible causes of the quality problem.

Remarkably, within forty-eight hours the troublesome components were identified, and within seven days shipments were again on stream. A new product was also ready for production.

The new CEO used the opportunity of the launch of the new product as a excuse for the shipment delays and the quality issue was quietly buried. Turnover surged ahead again and everyone breathed a sigh of relief.

However, one by one the old VPs were forced to resign and were replaced by the new president's own hand-picked managers. Despite the downturn in computer sales this company still prospers to this day under his absolute and unquestioned control.

This example illustrates that it takes a person of exceptional ability to hold on to his position after a rapid change in management, especially if the change has occurred as a result of a "chance event" of some kind. But a talented chief executive runs little risk of failure and the welfare of his entire organisation is secure in his competent hands.

Opportunists often ignore the attitude of workforce and management team

One important aspect of good management which is crucial, and which is rarely considered by the opportunist, is the ability to gain and keep the respect and cooperation of the workforce. Opportunists rarely appreciate the importance of the attitude of their workforce in their haste to seize the chance.

A lot of opportunist chief executives consider that the ordinary workers in a company are more or less irrelevant when planning their corporate coups. They just don't feature in any calculation of risk and reward. This type of CEO does not have the foresight to recognize the importance of the workers' support.

This is a grave error of judgement and I will discuss this later in more depth. But, for the time being, here is an example of how an able chief executive behaves when galvanizing his workforce. It deserves some careful scrutiny and should be imitated by any ambitious CEO who wants to be successful.

This is the case of the chief executive of a certain predatory company[7.2] which gained control of a new acquisition. The new CEO found that the company he had acquired had been in the hands of a weak and unintelligent management with a history of needlessly aggravating and ignoring its workforce's grievances. So there was plenty of pent-up resentment amongst the employees.

This neglect of the workforce by the old management had destroyed any trust or belief the workers had in the management. Credibility is, of course, the basis of any management's ability to manipulate or coerce its workforce. The company's previous policies had created a lot of division between the workers and the management. The management was universally distrusted and found that it had to negotiate with many different interest groups and trade unions. This made the company difficult to manage, and made implementing change almost impossible.

The new chief executive decided that strong management was required to bring a return to unity, peace and order in the company. He therefore placed a new general manager in day-to-day control of the company. This person was selected because he was both efficient and ruthless and he quickly succeeded in pacifying and uniting the workforce and management into a common fear and respect for him.

After six months this unifying process appeared to be complete. The chief executive now appointed a workers' representative to the board of directors (albeit with no significant power), and set up a workers' representative committee. He hinted to the workforce that he considered the measures employed by the general manager to be unfair and excessive, denying they were any of his own doing; he implied that the manager simply had an unsympathetic and autocratic personality!

41

One day he summoned the worker's representative to the head office without first informing the general manager and questioned him about the behaviour of the general manager. Very quickly the CEO found the evidence he needed - a case where the general manager had directly contradicted the CEO's explicit instructions. This provided the chief executive with a pretext. The next morning the general manager was summarily fired.

In his explanatory address to the workforce, the chief executive found (not to his surprise, of course) that he was addressing a unified and loyal workforce, delighted and grateful for his protection, and not the malcontent and disunited mob he had per force treated harshly by means of the ruthless general manager.

Controlling and manipulating the workers is, however, just one area of responsibility in which the able chief executive must excel. He must also be able to manipulate his management team and shareholders in a similar way. The following example illustrates just one strategy available to him.

The Lemmingson Group was a large domestic construction company whose chief executive was appointed by election with the support of a small but influential group of shareholders. This group was led by the chief executive's original sponsor, a particularly outspoken and long-standing shareholder. The new CEO was both efficient and ambitious. He was well-respected by all his employees except for some of the more traditionally-minded managers, but he was regarded with some suspicion by his board of directors and a considerable number of other shareholders. He was anxious to expand and diversify the company's activities into the high risk overseas timeshare construction business. When he outlined these plans to the board he was met with immediate resistance and scepticism from the older managers. In his efforts to get his own way, he turned to stratagem and would certainly have achieved his objectives had it not been for an unfortunate and unforeseeable turn of fate.

The new chief executive's major problem was how to get the support of enough shareholders. He also realized that underlying this problem was a lack of confidence in him by his management team. He dealt with these obstacles in four ways:

- He gradually fired, demoted, and discredited those in the original management team that opposed him, and thus deprived the major shareholders of access to any uncomplimentary reports about himself from inside the company.

- He gained both the support of and recognition by semi-state grant authorities which were sponsoring the company and providing essential financial assistance and encouragement for expansion.

- He began to ingratiate himself with a number of other small and influential shareholders with the help of his original sponsor, in order to win their support for his plans.

- He recruited and promoted a loyal management team which agreed with his expansion plans, and convinced the labour force of the value of his plans to them.

Under these circumstances any initial criticism of his schemes, either at board level or by the shareholders, could easily be discredited by simply quoting from the broadly based consensus of opinion which was (now) in his favour. From the shop-floor through the management team and large numbers of small shareholders, right up to the local authorities and government agencies, the CEO seemed to have supporters.

Everything appeared right for another assault on the big conservative shareholders to get their approval and fresh capital. However, the chief executive was unlucky. He only managed to complete three of the four strategies before his sponsor, the old shareholder, died unexpectedly.

The CEO, despite all his support, found himself left isolated without the essential shareholder support he had depended upon. None of the other supporters were so pivotal to the success of his plan as this shareholder and his supporters.

Gradually, the CEO's own health and enthusiasm began to fail under the continuous pressure of maintaining his position against his board and he began losing ground. Finally he lost all his support at board level. He was too late, the timing was wrong, the opportunity passed.

But he had achieved much in his time: he had fired all of the dissident and conservative middle-management he could identify, gained eminent respectability amongst the semi-state organisations, won the respect of the workforce for his "thoughtfulness" towards them, and he was surrounded by loyal and dedicated management. Still he had not achieved enough by the time his powerful enemies in the holding company board began to question his decisions and the amount of power he commanded. Fearing the inevitable, he was finally forced to resign.

---o0o---

9. Corporate acquisition by deception, crime or election

Means of gaining corporate control

Aside from opportunism and ability, the following techniques are frequently employed in company takeovers:

- Deception, criminal action or other dubious means.

- Election by the management or workers of a company, such as in a management buy-out or cooperative organisation.

The main issue for those considering fraudulent or criminal activity is the individual's ability to get away with his "misdeeds" and whether he can avoid civil or criminal prosecution or even prison.

Clearly these methods are the least attractive means of gaining control of a company with far too many unforeseeable risks and potentially unpleasant consequences, yet the takeovers of many companies, both great and small, is still conducted along unethical and fraudulent lines, and perpetrators are rarely brought to justice, in fact in Britain they are more likely to get a knighthood than a criminal record!

One could argue if there is no other way for the individual to achieve his objectives, and the risks are manageable, then why not?

The use of deceit or a criminal act

The following example is a mild illustration of this genre.

Piraprint Ltd., a two-year old small specialist printing company[8.1] was a partnership between three individuals: an accountant, an ambitious individual who had appointed himself the company's secretary and another working director who was made acting general manager. The original promoter of the idea was appointed managing director. In the early days of the partnership the company-secretary was given the task of registering the company and issuing shares as agreed by all. The company was immediately successful and showed tremendous growth potential. The two working directors were inundated with orders. Growth was so rapid that several refinancing actions were required to facilitate the unexpected business within the first eighteen months.

The company-secretary completed the company registration but never seemed to get around to issuing shares. All three partners were old friends so nobody was really concerned about this. They were all too busy anyway and the matter was always just pushed to the bottom of the agenda.

Business grew rapidly and before too long, major finance was required for expansion. The three partners had expected that this would happen eventually, but they had never really been too concerned to source the necessary funds, except the accountant who had negotiated a personal loan some months before. The chief executive, however, had already borrowed up to his own personal limit, taken a second-mortgage out on his home and waived his entitlement to a salary. Consequently he was absolutely unable to borrow any more money.

At a board-meeting the other two directors concluded that since he couldn't assist in financing the company anymore, it was unacceptable for him to remain as chief executive and they voted that he should resign. When he asked about his right to shares in the company, the accountant revealed that shares had not been issued to him, and thus he had no legal claim on the company. It was simply hard luck!

The chief executive had no option but to resign from his position. The accountant and the third director then issued themselves shares, a majority holding for the accountant and the remainder to his co-conspirator, along with the post of chief executive as a sweetener in return for his support and silence.

Gaining control by election

Let us turn to a more ethical route to the top, an elected CEO of some form of a "cooperative" company. The true cooperative is not a highly developed corporate form in western capitalism and election to the post of chief executive by one's peers, whether workers or managers, isn't very common.

In our context it isn't very interesting either because it is somewhat artificial and requires few of the skills for which we would normally award accolades for leadership or political manipulation. This method of acquisition does, however, deserve an example for those interested in the mechanics.

Carrigolgan Potteries Ltd., a ceramic manufacturer, had been suffering from severe financial troubles for some time. Sales had been gradually declining in the industry due to pressure from foreign imports and no new initiatives had been taken by the management to diversify or modernize. Factory closure seemed inevitable.

In an attempt to avert disaster, the chief executive initiated a wide-ranging redundancy plan. Naturally, the management and unions alike were outraged, feeling they were taking the blame for the company's low productivity. A bitter strike ensued. After two months of wrangling and fruitless negotiations, the board of directors met and decided that to sit out the strike was useless, and the time had come to put a stop to their losses. The factory was permanently closed and tenders invited for the purchase of the equipment.

A prominent member of the local branch of the union saw this as an opportunity. He was popular amongst his members and had worked hard for their interests. Seeing that the company's shareholders and board of directors had lost their nerve, he called a general meeting of all employees and suggested that the operation be taken over as a cooperative venture. The factory was situated in an area of high unemployment and the idea seemed attractive to everyone. Naturally, the union-leader was the obvious candidate to be the chief executive and he modestly accepted the popular nomination.

The factory was immediately occupied by the workers despite legal attempts by the shareholders to evict them, and it was quickly put back into production. Finally, the owners of the company, weary and unable to sell the business, gave way to the forceful union leader and local public opinion. They sold the assets and considerable liabilities of the company to the new cooperative for a nominal sum.

The workforce was exhilarated by their victory, and the union-leader was unanimously elected as permanent chief executive. As the company still had severe financial problems the workforce took half wages for many months, and the company secured state-assistance for its modernization plans.

47

Similarities between deception and election

So here we have a case of a CEO securing power by election. There are some similarities to the acquisition of power by deception or a criminal act because neither of these modalities actually require very much in the way of political and management skills or risk taking capacity. They rely more on opportunity and cunning than on cleverness and ability.

The Palace Coup

This technique is fraudulent, deceptive, and secretive. It works when an aspiring CEO seizes control of a company by engendering dissention against its incumbent chief executive in a so-called "Palace Coup". The new CEO removes an incumbent by garnering the support of a group of malcontents in the company's management.

The Palace Coup: Risks

Whilst the technique is a valid enough method to gain control, the new chief executive should reflect on the motives of those who assist him in this type of action. If their moves are based on discontent with the old management, the new CEO will only keep their support as long as he can satisfy their demands, and this is not always possible. The "plotters", now aware that they themselves have the power to dispose of a CEO, must themselves be removed and replaced as soon as possible by the new CEO.

In such circumstances it is better and safer for the new CEO to gain the support of those who were content and faithful under the old management than from those who sought to discredit and overthrow it. He should therefore eliminate his co-conspirators as soon as he has established his position in the new company, before they try to get rid of him!

---oOo---

10. Corporate acquisition from within

The second type of chief executive mentioned in the last chapter is the individual who is elected to his position with the consent of his fellows, either from within the management or from the labour force. This type of chief executive does not, as I have hinted, need a great deal of real ability, or be particularly opportunistic to succeed. He needs to be liked and respected by his peers and they must trust that he will protect their interests.

Internal acquisition

All corporate entities have managements and workforces and so there is always a risk that a company might be taken over from within in certain extreme circumstances. "Internal acquisition" has become quite a popular means of changing management in recent years, especially where a company is threatened with closure.

The key to determining who will be successful in these types of takeover is the attitude of the workforce towards individual members of the management. Very often the workforce will be highly influential in deciding who will become chief executive, and their choices may well be based on the treatment they received at the hands of individual members of the management previously.

The role of the workforce

A company's workforce is only really interested in two things: a reasonable wage and fair treatment from management with little bullying or coercion. On the other hand, a company's management almost always seeks to dominate and control their workforce - that's what managers do.

During the process of internal acquisition, these opposing aspirations of management and workforce can result in one of three scenarios, depending on the degree of trust and cooperation management has with its workforce and vice versa:

- A traditional stable oligarchic management - them and us.

- A stable cooperative organisation - we are all in this together.

- An unstable corporate conflict and anarchy - a testing of wills.

Possible outcomes

A traditional company with an oligarchic structure management is quite possible when the management and/or workforce feel comfortable with the traditional structure and have enough trusted candidates to take over the role of the oligarchs. In the case of a management buy-out, middle management, fearing the potential power of the workers, will try to seize the initiative to take over the company before any idea of cooperative management takes root amongst the workers. In this scenario, the existing management will usually move quickly to appoint one of their own number as chief executive, in order to protect their vested interests and status.

When mutual trust is impossible between the workforce and management, the workforce may prevail and appoint an individual or council of individuals to act as their representative during a domestic company takeover. Their hope will be that a workers' nominee will protect their interests.

Generally though, a take-over by the workers is uncommon. A company would have to be in an extremely sorry state for it to be taken over by its workforce, because if it had any real worth, the management would almost certainly have already manoeuvred to take it over for themselves. However, in the recent past, several companies, including mines, have been taken-over by their workers with some government support and a certain amount of success.

But let's move on from the mechanics of becoming chief executive to look at what faces the individuals concerned once they have gained power.

Risks to the CEO rest on where his support comes from

Any CEO that is appointed solely by the board of directors of a company will have a lot more problems holding onto power than one selected with the support of the workforce. This type of appointee starts from a position of distrust and maybe even open hatred, and consequently it is much harder for him to maintain control over the workforce, especially because the vested interests of the management are often at odds with those of the employees. This is often the case in a management buyout or similar change of power.

Conversely, a worker who manages to become the boss will find himself surrounded by those who consider themselves his equal. He has much less to fear from them than a manager appointed from the upper echelons. A popularly appointed CEO should be much more capable of managing and manipulating the workforce, even if he is also somewhat alienated from the upper layers of management team or board of directors.

Management buyouts

A management buyout can be thought of as a sort of commercial coup d'etat. A weak chief executive and/or board of directors are removed from power by disaffected members of their own management team. The new chief executive has to be very careful if he is not to meet the same fate as his ousted predecessor because he is, after all, still surrounded by those with proven predatory ability to remove unsatisfactory chief executives who don't act according to the wishes of the "coup leaders".

Risks from the workforce

The workers tend to be more honest in their intentions. Generally, they don't wish to dominate the management or manipulate the company's shareholders. They simply wish to have secure jobs and be free from subjugation from management.

A chief executive can never completely safeguard himself and his company's interests from a hostile workforce - they are too powerful by virtue of their numbers. On the other hand, a chief executive can generally remain immune from the malevolence of his own management. They are fewer in number and therefore more easily neutralized. The type and degree of threat posed, however, is quite different.

If a workforce is antagonistic, the most destructive action they can take is a strike, walk-out or work to rule, which although damaging, is more often a process of attrition than any kind of knockout blow. On the other hand, if elements of the management are hostile to the CEO they can bring about the spontaneous and total downfall of the chief executive and the company very quickly if given a chance. They have access to sensitive information, which put together with their apparent respectability, can be a fatal combination. Disgruntled or ambitious members of the management team are also in an excellent position to foresee opportunities to promote their own vested interests.

Managing other directors and managers

So we might come to the conclusion that the most dangerous colleagues for a CEO are his fellow directors!

Whilst it's almost always true to say that a company *must* have a workforce, it can also be said that most companies can manage for long periods of time *without* a lot of its management. After all, a chief executive can hire, fire, promote and demote middle management almost at will. He cannot *safely* do this with his workforce unless he wants to damage the basic productive capacity of the company.

There are some other considerations that a CEO must consider, the foremost of which is the strength of independence of each member of his management team.

Types of manager

Members of the management team fall into one of three classes:

- They either depend upon the chief executive for their position or they do not. If they are financially dependent, then they should be promoted and awarded the appropriate status and praise by the chief executive as loyal servants.

- Those who remain financially independent of the chief executive but are un-ambitious, apolitical or academically challenged can also still be used if they have some functional ability. They are no threat to the chief executive.

- Those who are ambitious, independent and selfish must be treated with the greatest suspicion because when the company experiences any kind of difficulty, they will grasp the opportunity to discredit the chief executive and promote their own interests.

Managing the workforce

A further consideration for the CEO is to maintain the support of the workforce. A CEO who has won endorsement and cooperation from his workforce must foster this backing.

This should be a simple matter because the workforce is much more easily manipulated than an intelligent management, plus they are also generally less personally ambitious and therefore pose less danger than the management team.

But, a chief executive who lacks the support of his workforce and solely relies on his managers and shareholders should, as a matter of priority, set about securing their cooperation.

There are various ways to nurture this support: inducing a feeling of greater security of employment, fair remuneration and generating a sense that management "care" about workers' welfare are some of the measures available.

When welcome changes to the employees' lives are seen and perceived to be the direct result of the CEO's intervention, a sense of tremendous obligation to the CEO will be generated. This is especially true when the workforce has been accustomed to mistreatment or has been ignored under a previous management regime.

This obligation by the workers in support of the CEO will be even greater than if the workers had supported the new CEO from the beginning, because he will be seen, not only as "decent" but also as a "liberator".

One way the chief executive can gain the support of his workers and keep them "on-side" is the use of employee participation schemes. Workers can luxuriate in the illusion of participation in the company's management by having a seat on the board. This is harmless enough and gives the impression to the workers that they have some control over their destiny. Then there are all kinds of small but important titbits: fringe benefits such as social events, sporting facilities and other small luxuries which gratify the workforce and keep them compliant. They all help.

Whichever way a chief executive attains power, he must have the cooperation and dedication of his workers. If he doesn't treat his workers decently, he will not have their support when it really matters. When a company experiences a commercial or other threat the CEO really depends on extra efforts from his workforce and he needs to be able to call in the favours he has granted over the years.

For example, when a company's market is threatened by cheap imports, a company may need to make substantial changes in work practices to increase productivity. If the workers don't respect and support the management team, there is no hope of this being possible. An obdurate workforce can block just about any management decision.

Management delegation and its risks

Most companies face a myriad of problems during periods of great upheaval and transition, such as in a take-over or management buyout. This instability lasts whilst the chief executive takes up the reins of control. During this time, the CEO must manage by means of delegation to fellow-directors and managers. There is an important consideration here.

When he delegates to his managers, the CEO's decisions are less potent than when his directors act on his orders. This is because a company's directors normally have the same vested interests in the success of the company whereas his managers may be envious and ambitious of the new CEO's position and may actually be working to damage the company. Parts of the management team may plot against the chief executive and they may ignore or dilute his orders if given a chance. In many other ways the managers may also seek to discredit the chief executive for the sake of their own personal interests[9.1]. This can be a very dangerous time for the CEO.

When a situation arises which seriously threatens the credibility of the chief executive, there will be no time for him to take absolute control. The entire organisation is based on devolved management, and the direct intervention of a CEO in the domain of a manager will be difficult because of the established rules of management protocol.

In these arduous times the new chief executive may well find it hard to retain trustworthy managers. When the company is operating in comfortable conditions there is never a shortage of faithful and dedicated supporters amongst the management, but when times are tough the CEO has few friends.

Keeping in touch with the workers

In this regard, a wise chief executive will ensure that he has a direct line of communications with his workforce, and that he has gained their trust and acknowledgement of their total dependence upon him personally.

Don't misunderstand my sentiments here, managers can usually be trusted, but they must always be watched. Workers cannot always be trusted, but they can always be easily subdued and manipulated. A rule which can be applied to the management of any organisation is: "Suspect your managers, placate your workers".

---oOo---

11. The measurement of corporate strength

Criteria to measure corporate strength

For most people, the most important characteristics of a company are its economic strength and self-confidence. Commerce is performance-orientated, and so the only way we can really judge a company's might and stamina is in reference to its ability to sustain its position and grow independently.

This calculation eventually comes down to a discussion of whether, in difficult times, a company's chief executive is managerially and financially competent enough to keep his company free of outside influences, does he and his co-directors have sufficient support from their own personnel to guide the company *independently* in difficult times, or does the CEO need external help (e.g. dilution of shareholding, etc.) if the going gets difficult?

How to remain independent

To remain independent, a chief executive must have sufficient personal capital (and/or access to funds or assets which can be readily liquidated) in order to discourage attacks from external or internal predators.

But, in addition to financial independence, the chief executive must be able to rely on the fidelity of his management team and the pliability and co-operation of his workforce, especially in difficult times. He should also be prepared. This means making appropriate financial and operational provisions for any future difficulties when the company is stable and profitable. But we will have more of this later. A chief executive's financial and personal commitments outside the company should be limited and easily liquidated in troubled times, so that he can concentrate on his mainstream commitments.

Repelling predators

If all these policies are taken on board, then corporate predators (internal or external) are far less likely to attempt to damage the chief executive, or exploit the difficulties of the company to take control. People generally dislike taking unnecessary risks, especially when they are likely to encounter stiff resistance from a well resourced adversary. Such would be the case when a company has a loyal management and workforce and a strong chief executive who is known to have substantial personal resources.

A chief executive who makes these preparations for his company's defence will also gain respect from his employees, so naturally they will comply with his requests more willingly, even when there is no particular threat. People feel more secure and confident when they feel sure they can trust in the prudence and good governance of "the boss". Provided a chief executive maintains these policies and he remains calm and consistent, there is no corporate problem that cannot be solved.

But there are some people who object to this strategy. They argue that employee loyalty, cooperation and financial independence are just not enough to protect the CEO against a really determined opponent.

Dealing with opposition

In the event of serious financial or other corporate trouble, there will always be fears of job losses and cutbacks amongst the workforce. A CEO in these circumstances may well have to sell these kinds of austerity measures to the workers. He may not always have the backing of his management for they are constantly ready to betray him out of self interest, but a strong and intelligent chief executive will prevail against all objections. He will always be able to point out to his workforce that the current troubles are nothing in comparison with what would happen if he had to close the company down completely and make all of them redundant - management included.

But if the opposition continues, the chief executive must take swift and irrevocable action against the resistance. He is very well placed to do this and he should carefully manage who is removed or dismissed. The CEO's actions should suggest that the job losses of these few were "designed to protect the job security of the many", and the company's future. The workforce will soon come to believe that any unpopular actions were a necessary part of the company's survival, and therefore the chief executive will actually be seen as the protector of their interests, i.e. the interests of the survivors.

Maintaining the confidence of the workforce

After serious corporate restructuring or economic privations, it is important that the confidence of the workforce in the CEO and his management team remains strong during the recovery. The company's workforce are going to have to place still further trust in the CEO, so it's very important that they trust him to get them out of trouble.

Ironically, the sacrifices of the workforce will, in time, place them under an even greater obligation to the chief executive. People often feel under a greater obligation for what they give than for what they receive. It should, therefore, not be difficult for a prudent chief executive to inspire his employees to withstand and recover from any crisis if he sticks to the simple rules above.

---o0o---

12. State-corporations, civil service and governments

The importance of state organisations to the CEO

I propose to deal briefly here with the role of a chief executive in the management structure of state and civil service organisations[11.1] and with the relationship between private commercial organisations and government. There are many good reasons for a chief executive to understand state organisations and how commercial corporations should deal with them. One must comprehend the way state bureaucracies operate before being able to devise methods to utilize their considerable power to one's benefit.

The management of state-controlled organisations

In the case of state-controlled companies and the civil service, the problems of management faced by a new chief executive are quite different from those in the commercial world. Generally the problems of the organisation are inherited and have become established long before any CEO takes up his position.

These types of organisation are not managed by individuals who are necessarily either opportunistic or particularly able. Mediocrity and inaction is more important in these organisations than talent. They tend to be managed by people who have demonstrated their ability to tolerate inefficiency without worrying too much about it.

State CEOs versus corporate CEOs

Since these are state-funded institutions, no matter how the chief executive behaves, within reason, these institutions will keep him in office for his full term and he will rarely be criticised by colleagues or anyone else that matters, however badly he or 'his' company performs.

These chief executives do not need to defend their organisations against any outside predators, competitors, or the usual financial and commercial threats. Nor do they have to concern themselves too much with controlling their workforce because long-established and accepted infrastructures and codes of practice exist to keep everyone in "their place".

In addition, there is no ultimate "consequence of error" of the kind we find in commercial entities. If the civil service doesn't perform, it doesn't, for instance, go bankrupt. It simply covers up its losses and quietly continues as if nothing has happened.

In state controlled organisations there are virtually no circumstances in which a chief executive will lose his job or irretrievably damage his corporation. Indeed, job security is so great, that a chief executive and his many subordinates are really only interested and concerned with their own upward movement within the hierarchy. This and other little perks become much more important to them than the efficient running of their organisation. This general disinterest and lack of accountability explains the legendary incompetence of the civil service and other state "companies".

Because these organisations are fundamentally underpinned by the ultimate authority of the state, there is little to be said about their management and control. However, their manifest proliferation in number and influence in recent years means they must be understood and taken seriously by real commercial CEOs who may have to deal with them for all kinds of reasons.

Dealing with state organisations

Thus, however little respect we may have for these organisations, it is important for the chief executive of a private company to remember that he must maintain a very close relationship with all government or statutory bodies. Whatever aspersions we may cast upon them, we need to do that in private and not show any disrespect to their management face to face.

After all, these people make and enforce the laws which eventually govern the CEO's activities, so he needs to look after them carefully. A successful CEO must not lose sight of the fact that to attain his goal he must manage his dealings with these organisations very carefully indeed.

There are, of course, many ways of getting one's own way with governments, such as using commercial lobbying groups, making donations to the right political party (or all of them!), and looking after the local legislators and councillors "at Christmas", so to speak, with carefully delivered gifts and favours.

And there are plenty of ways of punishing them if they don't respond sensibly or if they become a little overzealous. But we won't dwell on these methods and I leave the rest to the fertile imagination of the astute chief executive.

---oOo---

13. Management organisation and the use of consultants

Up to now we have discussed the types and characteristics of various commercial and government corporations and organisations, the reasons why they succeed or fail, and the methods used in acquiring and maintaining control of them. It now remains to discuss how these companies should organize themselves for their own protection and corporate expansion.

We have already concluded that a company, whether old or new, must be founded on strong management, and that this management should centre on an independent, courageous and forceful chief executive. He, in turn, must not be afraid of imposing his will or be squeamish about hard-headed decisions when necessary. When the ability to impose the management's will is evident, then sensible and compliant conduct by the company's employees will naturally follow.

Enforcing management decisions

Let us direct our attentions to the actual mechanics of enforcing the will of the chief executive and take a look at the kind of people whom he should select to help him in this task.

There are many human resources available to a chief executive in the defence of his position and his company. He has his management team, external management consultants, his company auditors and various state advisory bodies.

Beware of management consultants

Of these three latter organisations, management consultants and state advisory bodies are the most useless and dangerous. If a chief executive bases his decisions on the recommendations of these people, he will never achieve lasting security or stability and I will now explain in some detail why this is[12.1].

Management consultants and their ilk are employed on a fee-basis. They are usually anxious to prolong their contracts and drag out problems they are supposed to solve. Whilst they may be considered capable by their professional peers, they are frequently undisciplined with no loyalty to anyone except themselves. Complacent and cynical, they usually prove to be quite incompetent when faced with real world problems and prefer to operate on the basis of avoiding confrontation for as long as possible.

The attitudes of external management consultants often aggravate personnel confrontations, making it harder to resolve problems.

In addition, they are notoriously expensive, so much so that their fees often negate any value derived from their frequently negligible contribution to a company's well-being.

Indeed, most international consultants calculate their charges based not on the likely reasonable cost of a client's project, but on what they consider they can get away with!

Why management consultants are worthless

The advice of these "experts" is so paltry because of the underlying avarice of the individuals working for these management consultancies. They are driven by personal gain and their only loyalty is to their own bank balance.

Most consultancies will not assist a client in severe financial difficulties by delaying payment of fees for a while as they fear non payment.

This behaviour by these ambulance chasers of the financial world is deplorable, for the client may be in his moment of greatest need.

Just to illustrate the risks of employing management consultants, let us briefly look at the consultant's own management and relationship with a client company.

Either a management consultancy has an ability to assist a client company or they do not. If they do have that ability, then they are not to be trusted because they will be privy to confidential and potentially damaging information concerning their clients.

If they do not have any management ability, then they are, at best, useless, whilst at worst they can destroy a client's company by incompetence in fields as delicate as industrial relations and marketing management.

So there really are no circumstances in which one should ever trust or employ a management consultancy, because they are either dangerous or useless.

For example, take the case of a well-known international consultancy which managed within three weeks to escalate a small productivity problem in the three thousand strong workforce of a large nylon manufacturer into a disastrous year long, all-out strike, ultimately leading to the total and final closure of the plant. The consultant's gross ineptitude and extreme arrogance took the company's industrial relations into freefall, antagonizing the company's workforce and alienating its management.

The consultancy collected its fee and left the project and the company in a state of total collapse. This is no isolated event. Corporate histories are full of such stories, though most victims are too embarrassed to admit such expensive errors of judgement.

Alternatives to management consultants

So the CEO is better advised to use internal consultancy whenever possible and be as self-reliant on the company's own internal skills as is practical. Internally conducted projects where the chief executive has much more control over the conduct of participating managers don't normally carry the same risks or costs as similar projects using external consultancies.

We can legitimately ask the questions: Isn't it better for a chief executive to rely upon his own ability and resources? Shouldn't he rely more on the intimate knowledge and dedication of those he knows and trusts, those who know their own predicament more than any outsider, i.e. his own management team? It is self evident that self reliance is the answer. I apologize for my rhetorical questions.

Naturally the management consultant hastens to differ, claiming management cannot "see the wood from the trees". This may be the case, but rather than trust the judgement of outsiders, there are other ways a CEO and his management can overcome their hurdles. There is no need to hire mercenaries.

To be fair, it must be admitted management consultants can occasionally deliver some small improvements to a company's health, (provided they are constantly and carefully supervised), however, they can and frequently do instigate rapid and spectacular disasters, generally speaking they just aren't worth the risk.

14. Dependence and self-reliance

There are other types of ineffective and hazardous consultancy agencies which can be sought from state and commercial advisory bodies.

State advisory bodies

These organisations usually obtain better results than independent management consultants but the downside is they are much more likely to betray a client's confidence within an industry, including to his competitors.

If they are unsuccessful a lot of resources and time will have been wasted. If they are successful, then the client's company will be the subject of continuous quotation by these organisations to other prospective clients, including of course, his competitors.

Risks in inviting external advice

Some manufacturing industries have such similar processes and equipment that engineering and productivity data are literally interchangeable between companies. It is very common to see this standard data, once established by a consultant in a client's company, sold repeatedly to other customers. Consultants justify this by citing its continued use by the original client. The same risks exist within the service industries where operational methods and markets are remarkably similar.

Thus the close links within the industry make this type of consultant even more dangerous than the independent management type. At least independent consultants can be vetted. Semi-official consultants, on the other hand, are appointed as a ready made team by the advisory body without much opportunity for executive vetting and weeding out of untrustworthy members of the team. Allowing this type of interference in the management of a company is certainly not a demonstration of a chief executive's self-reliance and is a perilous path to tread.

As a rule, a chief executive should never seek assistance from outside his company. He should have enough faith in his own experience and management. Any company which cannot take care of its own problems is condemned to reliance upon others, and ultimately to failure.

Manage your own risks and adversities

The chief executive who doesn't acknowledge or foresee adversity is incompetent. But few chief executives are capable of such unemotional realism and corporate self-analysis.

Many commercial problems are ignored or remain undetected until a catastrophe actually occurs. There are plenty of examples of companies falling into needless bankruptcy because of a simple inability by the CEO and his management to see what was obviously wrong within a company. If we look at the recent history of such unfortunate organisations, we can often observe a plethora of consultancies working for them. This is a real sign of poor corporate health.

Instead of using these "corporate leeches", a chief executive would be better advised to spend his time and money motivating his own managers and applying his own skills to understand and deal with the company's problems.

It is this first fatal move to dependence upon others that signals the demise of a company, and it is a sure indication of the lack of competence and confidence of the chief executive.

Other types of dependency

Finally, another form of attachment to be studiously avoided is too much reliance on other companies, such as competitors, customers or credit institutions like banks.

Remaining independent of business competitors is straightforward enough, the CEO should just refuse all businesses connections. Dependence upon customers is a subtler and more complex problem, the solution lies in building a wide and diverse customer base. Successfully avoiding dependence on the money lenders is a much more formidable task however, requiring an iron will and exceptional financial planning skills.

Dominance by large customers

It is classically dangerous for a small company supplying a large international corporation to become too dependent upon that single large customer. The small supplier gradually comes to rely upon this customer for all their business, thus becoming utterly susceptible to the will of this customer's management.

A large customer will inevitably make all kinds of demands on a small company, insisting on credit and setting the rules for purchasing. If the small supplier wishes to keep the account, the small supplier will be forced to satisfy every whim of his overbearing customer. The chief executive of such a small supplier company eventually ceases to be in control of his own business.

Don't appear too attractive to the competition

Other corporate predators may cast an avaricious eye on a chief executive's company. For this there is one golden rule: never appear as too attractive a proposition to the outside world. A chief executive must suppress his corporate ego in order to avoid any unwelcome advances.

The so-called poison pill method is an ideal way of doing this. In this strategy, a chief executive takes on (or gives the impression of saddling the company with) large extra liabilities and debt. This discourages "corporate raiders" from making an attempt to gain control of the company. Of course, the liabilities must be shed after potential threats have passed.

Stay independent

In conclusion, I cannot emphasize enough that, unless a chief executive can manage his own corporate affairs by relying upon himself and his own personnel, his company is not secure. By turning to outsiders the company will always be dependent, more or less, upon chance opportunities and the will of others, rather than upon the confidence, strength and ability of the chief executive. It will always be weak and at risk.

---oOo---

15. The chief executive and his management team

The roles and responsibilities of the CEO

In this section we are going to conclude the discussion about how a prudent chief executive should deal with his management. We will also attempt to clarify the roles of the chief executive and his managers, their areas of responsibility and the skills which each should possess.

HR management

On a day-to-day basis, a chief executive should dedicate himself to human motivation, manipulation of his employees and the administration of discipline against anyone defying his decisions. These practices are what are expected of a chief executive by his employees. Any other skill he may have is considered just an extra bonus.

These human resource management skills shouldn't be underestimated. They are vitally important, not only because they keep the chief executive in control, but also because they are the means by which the ambitious CEO acquires that control in the first place. Also, as we have already said, a chief executive has to keep an eye out for ambitious colleagues around him. They might just be the next CEO in waiting!

Routine management, boring but essential

However, not all CEOs are that motivated to do what is required to keep their position. Many chief executives are more interested in gratifying themselves at the expense of the company. They prefer to enjoy the company's profits and their personal benefits, avoiding the daily grind of business problems rather than actually running their company. However, they neglect their duties and these essential skills at their peril.

A good chief executive must be capable of dealing with the constant difficulties of business life, the daily bread and butter issues in management, not only to survive, but also to affirm his authority over those who surround him. If he shirks from this duty, he will be universally despised by his employees, his competitors and his management.

Maintaining respect for the CEO

It is vital to be aware of the importance of this phenomenon. There is simply no comparison between a chief executive who directs from a position of strength and confidence and one who cannot.

It is unrealistic to expect employees and members of the management to respect or cooperate with a weak CEO, or that a feeble CEO will be safe in the presence of employees that have minimal regard for him. An ineffectual chief executive will always be nervous of the strong influences swirling and circling around him and will never be able to trust his employees or management. In these circumstances a weak CEO will quite rightly be held in contempt by his people.

Be prepared

In periods of corporate stability a prudent chief executive should devote his time to exercises in crisis management, risk analysis, and problem-solving. He should work together with his managers through scenarios and simulations of how they intend to cope with problems involving industrial relations, marketing, cash flow problems, credit squeezes, market changes and the management of change in general. This practice will stand the company in good stead when trouble really does come.

Understand "the field"

To be effective a chief executive must be intimately aware of the company's position in the market. He should have a good understanding of the market and its direction, and above all, a good CEO must understand the mechanisms of bringing about corporate change. The ability to be flexible is all important and will assist the chief executive and his management team in dealing with crises when they arise. In addition, these skills will improve his ability to expand the company since the same knowledge and crafts are required to deal with both crisis and opportunity.

Learn by example

A prudent chief executive should take an active interest in the history of commercial and industrial management. He should understand how prominent and successful chief executives of the past achieved their goals and why they suffered reverses. This will help him emulate the decisions of the former and avoid the mistakes of the latter.

In summary, a chief executive should remind himself and his managers constantly that a time of stability is not a time to relax, but rather an opportunity to be used assiduously in preparation for withstanding adversity, as well as for implementing plans for expansion.

---o0o---

16. What brings the chief executive credit or discredit?

Forming a CEO's public image

I would now like to discuss how a chief executive should manage his public image. This includes how he behaves towards his closest associates and confidants, how he deals with his employees and how he manages public opinion about himself. In so doing, I will touch on what we traditionally refer to as the "virtues and qualities" in an individual's personality.

Morality versus reality

On this delicate subject, I will try to be completely honest and realistic rather than take an idealistic or moral position. We all know that there is a major difference between human morality and actual behaviour. It is delusory to make decisions based on the premise that man's behaviour is guided by high moral values. Failure to acknowledge the inherent traitorous and selfish nature of human beings is the first step on the road to self-destruction. Being realistic about human failings is the first step towards self-preservation!

For example, a person who tries to act honourably, all the time and in all respects, will inevitably come to grief. This is simply because he is surrounded by so many who behave dishonourably, and do so constantly without scruples or hesitation. A chief executive wishing to maintain his position must learn how to be dishonourable when it is necessary and must understand under what circumstances being unprincipled is appropriate. Our CEO must be capable of dressing up dishonour as pragmatism.

What attracts public acclaim to the CEO?

The very nature of the chief executive's job means he is in the spotlight more than most; consequently his behaviour will be a topic ripe for discussion and commentary by his employees.

Virtues and Vices: Let us make a list of positive and corresponding negative adjectives, virtues and vices that may frequently be used in reference to the character of our dear leader. For no particular reason we will place the virtues in alphabetical order!

Virtues	Vices
assertive	timid
compassionate	hard-hearted
contented	jealous
economical	frivolous
generous	stingy, mean
honest	duplicitous, tricky, cunning, untrustworthy
inspiring	lacklustre
kind	nasty
lenient	harsh
modest	arrogant
memorable	forgettable
pragmatic	unrealistic
resolute	indecisive
strong	weak
thoughtful	inconsiderate
unique	common

In the ideal world our executive would possess all of the qualities in the left-hand column and none in the right. However, expedience demands that the chief executive cannot afford such a high moral code, the very nature of modern commerce precludes it and indeed the observance of such niceties may cost him his company.

Popularity versus expedience

Let me make it plain, I am not advocating that a chief executive should set out to be deliberately unethical or immoral. But a chief executive must be careful not to make his decisions based solely on moral considerations. He also shouldn't pander to popular opinion by trying to exhibit those attributes which are generally considered to make him a "good man".

A chief executive, who overlooks his objectives in favour of winning the support of public opinion, may well be contributing to his own downfall. He should, where possible avoid the vices above but if he sometimes has to, for example, appear hard-hearted, then it won't be of great significance because it won't affect his status. Behaving weakly, however, in order to appear virtuous, could well undermine the CEO's position entirely.

In conclusion, the chief executive mustn't be timid, for instance, demonstrating reluctance to take steps to enhance his position or benefit the company simply because he may be accused of being dishonourable or unethical. Indeed, if he sticks rigidly to some of the qualities that most people consider to be virtuous, he will probably be instrumental in the company's eventual destruction!

In the same way, and in some cases, the practice of some of the vices enumerated above may well promote the prosperity and success of the CEO and his company. It is no accident there are several adjectives describing the opposite of straightforward, honest conduct! The CEO's behaviour, therefore, depends on the situation, rather than any moral notion of honour imposed on him from outside.

---oOo---

17. Generosity versus meanness

Is generosity good in business?

Let us now look in more detail at these "qualities", and how a chief executive should formulate his policy towards them. We will begin with "generosity".

Everyone would agree that it is splendid for a chief executive to have a reputation for generosity. Nevertheless, if a CEO really deserves a reputation for "generosity", then he is almost certainly heading for trouble.

This is because if the largesse is sincere, it will probably be quite modest and will pass completely unnoticed. He is hardly going to give away significant parts of his wealth unless his name is Bill Gates, of course. The CEO's charitable sentiments and actions will be quite minor and will not protect him from being accused of meanness at a later stage. If a chief executive really wishes to be known for his generosity, he must be frequently and ostentatiously lavish and make sure everyone knows about it.

Too much generosity

Another consideration here is that gifts or favours given frequently lose their significance in the eyes of the recipients. They will not be as greatly valued as the occasional reward. Employees become complacent about a chief executive's generosity and he will constantly have to increase the value and frequency of his favours if they are to remain effective. This contributes further still to the drain on a company's finances and limits the rewards that a chief executive can bestow when it is really necessary.

Naturally, from time to time it is necessary to award favours to employees who have given exemplary service or to placate those who feel aggrieved. However, if the chief executive has a policy of indiscriminate generosity he will soon have nothing 'special' to offer when the time calls for gifts or favours to facilitate action.

An over generous chief executive rapidly dissipates valuable resources for no return. When he can no longer afford to be so bountiful, he will, of course, have to stop the hand-outs and try to recover the cost of his earlier extravagances in some other way, such as cutbacks of some kind. This will cause even more resentment. It would have been better if the chief executive had not been so unnecessarily lavish in the first place.

Generosity, in whatever form, has to be paid for eventually. When the day of reckoning comes, instead of being perceived as being open-handed, the chief executive will, more than ever, be considered mean for curtailing favours to employees and other "retainers".

Generosity versus meanness

Men are always quicker to condemn those in power than to defend them, more likely to see a chief executive as stingy than to remember him when he was philanthropic.

If a chief executive cannot afford to maintain his generosity at a level which will win him the reputation he desires, he must just learn to live with the reputation of being mean. In time, this policy will be understood or at least accepted by the company's employees and come to be respected as prudent.

A prudent CEO will be seen to have protected the security of the company, to have encouraged its expansion and maintained its independence. These interests are more important in the long run, both for the employees and the chief executive, than any temporary pretensions to benevolence.

In reality a chief executive is seen as generous by those from whom he takes nothing, and this is the majority of his employees. He is only condemned as mean by those to whom he gives nothing, and these are few.

Many blue chip companies pay seemingly extravagant salaries to entice top-quality senior personnel to work for them, but these same companies are rarely generous with the colossal profits generated as a result of the efforts of these personnel[16.1]. The banking and IT industries are prime examples of this. The lavishness towards senior bankers extends only as far as it is necessary to generate huge profits for the shareholders of the banks and does not permeate down to the vast rank and file of employees.

In conclusion, a wise chief executive shouldn't pay any attention to whether he is labelled generous or stingy by public opinion, it is more important for him to maintain sufficient wealth to defend the company and his position in times of trouble with the minimum amount of disruption.

Selective generosity

Whilst a CEO may have gained his position by a reputation for largesse, it doesn't follow that he must or can maintain his position by more of the same! A prudent chief executive should be open-handed with the rewards of his company's improved productivity with those retainers that have helped him achieve the gains. This profit has been realised by management ability and sharing some of it will act as a source of encouragement to senior and other key employees.

The use of such incentives is quite a different matter to gratuitous "generosity"; if such munificence is practised thoughtlessly, the chief executive will lose the ability to use generosity strategically, and its practice will weaken the company financially.

To avoid this, a good CEO must be capable of rapacity and tolerate being disliked for it.

---oOo---

18. Cruelty versus compassion: Is it better to be feared or liked?

Being liked by your employees

The "quality" of compassion and the "evil" of cruelty are more important considerations to a chief executive than the "virtue" of generosity.

It is certainly more important for a chief executive to have a public reputation for sympathy rather than being known for his heartlessness.

The main condition here is that a CEO's reputation for compassionate behaviour should not be allowed to interfere in his actions, the wellbeing of the CEO and his company always "trumps" any sentimental feelings of pity.

As with all the other so-called vices, the chief executive must be just as careful not to abuse his application of kindness and hard-heartedness in his day to day management decisions. In addition, he must also avoid being seen as callous when it is not appropriate or conversely overly empathetic when it is not necessary.

Being cruel to be kind

There are times when ruthlessness is necessary in management. Often an action which appears heartless at the time will come to be seen as quite fair or even truly compassionate at a later date.

Thus, a chief executive shouldn't worry too much if he incurs reproach for an act of apparent callousness, provided he is confident that it is in the interest of the company's security, and that his action will not inadvertently disaffect his retainers and employees when he is need of their support.

Making an occasional example of a miscreant employee is ultimately a more compassionate act than misguided attempts to appear tolerant whereby the CEO allows disorder, waste and disrespect for the company's rules and its chief executive. This type of "compassion" damages an entire organisation whereas an occasional dismissal or disciplinary action against an individual only affects the individual. The end justifies the means.

Starting out with the right image

However, a new chief executive often finds it difficult to avoid a reputation as a 'hard man' because of the many difficulties and suspicions he encounters when taking up his new position. He must tread carefully at first; avoid making rash decisions and becoming irrationally distrustful of those around him or antagonising those whom he may need to become established.

Is it better to be liked than feared?

The answer must be that one would like to be both but because it is nearly always impossible to combine these attributes satisfactorily, it is usually better to be feared than liked.

Human fickleness

The cynic in us may generalize that human beings are usually fair-weather friends.

When conditions are favourable, most employees are dedicated to their chief executive and there is nothing they wouldn't do for him or the company, but if there is any personal threat they will protect their own interests first.

Any chief executive that comes to rely entirely upon "friendly" promises of fidelity made by his retainers during "good times" and has not taken the necessary precautions to protect both himself and the company during times of difficulty is inviting trouble.

Such proclamations of "friendship" are essentially encouraged by the superior financial standing and status of a chief executive. Such relationships are not based on either real respect or fear and will crumble when times of trouble rock the company.

Why, how and when fear is better than friendship

Men concern themselves less with injuries they cause to a likeable fellow than to someone they fear. The main reason for this is the much greater dread of punishment. Therefore, a wise CEO will use fear to protect himself from injury.

But some subtlety is needed here. A chief executive must make himself feared in such a way that, if he is not liked he does not generate outright hatred in his employees and retainers. There is a clear distinction here.

Avoiding hatred and resentment

For example, a CEO can avoid hostility by respecting his employees' abilities and rewarding them for their dedication and hard work. When a hard decision is necessary it must be swift, surgical, non-negotiable and finite, leaving no long-running resentments. The chief executive must carefully plan and think out the implications of a coercive action before he carries it out.

For example, in the event of a necessary dismissal, it should only be carried out when there is an absolute justification for it. Once this is established, however, the termination must take place at once.

In such an event, it must be explained to everyone that it is better to dismiss an incompetent or untrustworthy employee than to allow the company and everyone else's jobs (or salaries) to be threatened by a "weak link" or a "disruptive" influence.

Whereas people soon forget their old colleagues, they rarely forget a pay-cut or a missed promotion. In times of difficulty a chief executive should not worry about seeming or indeed being hard-hearted, because that is what is expected of him in his efforts to maintain the unity, security and discipline of the company.

Employee termination - being hard-headed

Employee termination is a difficult issue and a delicate subject for every CEO. Few chief executives manage this part of their responsibilities very well.

Why is it that so many executives and managers take so long to reach the final decision to dismiss an employee? Senior management often deliberate endlessly before finally acknowledging that they have to fire some hapless figure. Usually this period of "consideration" is filled with a great deal of painful discussion and hand wringing about the offending individual.

This kind of indecisive behaviour doesn't stem from lack of management experience (or even experience in dismissing an employee). Often the same reticent chief executives are quite decisive and efficient in all other aspects of business. So what is it about terminating an employee that makes many CEOs squeamish?

Candidates for a management position are often asked if they have ever fired anyone, as if such experience proves the maturity of a management candidate.

In addition, many managers and chief executives need considerable provocation before they will terminate an employee. Lack of performance or infidelity to the company is often not enough. Even gross misconduct or dishonesty is barely sufficient.

What is it then that causes this reticence to dismiss an employee? Is it good for a chief executive to be so cautious?

Generally, managers and executives are reluctant to dismiss employees because they harbour some misplaced sympathy for the employee or they fear that they will gain a reputation for harsh management, or they feel some self-doubt about the correctness of their decision, a lack of self-confidence.

Employee termination - how NOT to do it

Generally speaking, the first reaction of an executive when an employee fails to measure up to expectations is to examine if it is the executive's own fault. He wonders if he has failed to communicate properly with the employee, if the staff member was properly trained or if he had been correctly assigned in the company. At this stage the executive doesn't confront the employee with his doubts, this is his first mistake.

Next, the weak chief executive turns to structural changes in his organisation, i.e. moving employees around, making allowances for the miscreant's shortcomings and rescheduling work to accommodate him. At this stage the CEO simply cannot face the reality that he is going to have to fire the staff member.

If after all these prevarications the employee still does not respond, then gradually the trust between the executive and the employee becomes irretrievably broken. If the chief executive doesn't terminate him or her at this stage, a torturous period of aggression and anguish will follow for both parties. The previously informal contact between the two becomes impossible. The executive sees the employee as a resentful "viper in his bosom" whilst the employee, by this time detecting that something is badly amiss, feels persecuted and keeps his head down, so much so that he performs even more badly and may thus compound the felony. This combination of broken faith, distrust and enmity makes for a most unpleasant and counter-productive environment for everyone, making both employee and CEO angry and frustrated.

Finally the situation becomes intolerable for the chief executive and the painful psychological decision to terminate is finally made. However, having prevaricated this much, there is nothing to stop the executive delaying execution for a little longer and he begins a further, final soul-searching period.

The CEO starts to examine all the personal barriers against termination, such as the employee's family, his health, his past service, his job prospects, the pain it will cause him etc. Inextricably connected with this is the terminator's self-pity and fear of admission of personal failure, implied by the dismissal of an employee recruited under his regime.

When it finally comes to dismissal, the tension evaporates with verbal recriminations and insults from the hapless employee. At this moment the weak chief executive will invariably extend a golden handshake to both quieten the employee's anger and satisfy the executive's conscience that he has compensated the employee adequately.

What I have described above is how NOT to terminate an employee. The upheaval and distress caused as a result of the chief executive's lack of resolve is enormous and all pervasive. It has not benefited the employee, the company, the CEO or his image amongst the remaining staff as a decisive boss.

When it comes to dismissing an employee, make the decision carefully, harbour no misgivings or discussion and execute the decision at once. Its better for all concerned.

Employee termination - a rule of thumb

The golden rule in dismissal (and many other business decisions) is: "If it must be done, then it is best to do it quickly, however unpleasant". Any chief executive who doesn't apply this policy is merely inviting contempt, cultivating resentment and encouraging corporate chaos by demonstrating both a lack of decisiveness and clarity of action.

Ruthlessness, brutality and restraint

One might wonder how a chief executive manages to maintain his position after periods of adversity when he may have been obliged to adopt harsh measures, act dishonourably, fraudulently or dishonestly, without getting a bad reputation for any of the above.

Here, I believe, we are really dealing with the appropriate use of ruthlessness. We must realize that it is an acceptable and indeed important characteristic of an effective management.

However there is one important caveat to this statement: ruthless actions are only effective and safe when they are used once and for all, and have the objective of establishing or maintaining a secure and lasting company and management. Harsh measures should not be persisted in, but simply used to gain advantage and protect the interests of the company as a whole.

Continuous ruthlessness is counter-productive. It is corrosive to the moral of a company and ceases very rapidly to be effective. It is a great error of judgement for a chief executive to adopt a strategy which includes the continuous coercion of his employees.

CEOs that act tough and then moderate their stance having achieved their objective have an opportunity to consolidate their position and give their employees a chance to forgive and forget. But those who adopt severe management techniques as their normal standard of practice give rise to a culture of hatred and resentment and this only serves to undermine the security of the CEO and the prosperity of the company.

It is easy to inspire the hatred of other people, a clever CEO can be single-minded when necessary but without inspiring long-lasting loathing.

Ruthlessness, heartlessness and decisiveness

Having decided when a chief executive must NOT be hard-nosed, let us now examine the situations when it is expedient to be merciless or ruthless.

After a chief executive takes up his position, his first task should be to establish which of his employees need to be disciplined, demoted or dismissed. He must take these actions with complete resolve, and he must take them immediately.

At all costs a CEO must avoid having to take continuous punitive action over a long period. If he adopts a decisive (seemingly ruthless) policy, the chief executive will assure everyone that these changes in personnel and the accompanying traumas are over, once and for all. He can then get on with the more important business of gaining positive support from his workforce and managers. He can do this, as I have said, by means of selective favouritism, conferring benefits and promotion.

The chief executive who does not act in a decisive way because he is badly advised or afraid of being accused of callousness, will always be on the defensive and he will never be able to depend upon his workforce or management. They will always perceive the CEO as weak and indecisive.

Avoiding management by attrition

If a CEO doesn't confront unpopular and difficult decisions at once and act with a degree of cold single-minded efficiency, he will certainly end up dealing with his problems in a piecemeal way, and his employees will always be the target of his unresolved attempts to maintain stability. They will therefore always feel insecure because they will never know when or against whom the chief executive will strike next. This gives rise to a long-drawn out and ultimately unsuccessful "management by attrition". This is absolutely the wrong way to maintain the cooperation of a workforce and is good for nothing.

When, however, the violence of the take-over or a corporate re-organisation is a discreet and final event and the reasons are explained to everyone, then at least the remaining survivors will soon forget the chief executive's actions, and any resentment they may feel at the time will soon be dissipated.

Dealing with the aftermath of corporate blood-letting

After a period of "brutality" such as a corporate take-over, a CEO will need to quickly restore stability and trust, which will mean comforting the surviving employees and restoring goodwill by dishing out benefits to some of them.

This benevolence must be a gradual, careful process since the chief executive needs time to consider who he will select for promotion etc. Above all, a chief executive must be consistent in his behaviour, regardless of the condition of the company at any time.

Most importantly, a CEO needs to confer benefits selectively. In difficult times when there is little time for discipline and careful management consideration, benefits awarded to employees are often viewed as acts of desperation and, above all, are taken as a sign of weakness. Therefore the CEO should make haste slowly in this period, his decisions will be better and his management will be perceived to be considered rather than forced by circumstances.

Conclusion

In conclusion, since most people will like or dislike their chief executive according to their personal preferences, it is up to the chief executive if he wants to foster a climate of fear. A chief executive cannot stop his employees from disliking him, but he can formulate policies which will persuade them not to hate or resent him, even if they do fear him.

---o0o---

19. Honouring one's word, when and how?

Honour in theory and practice

Common morality states that everyone must honour their word at all times. In business, many transactions are based on the giving of one's word. Indeed, it is most praiseworthy for a chief executive to honour his word, be straightforward in his dealings and avoid deceit and deviousness. All this is true in theory!

However, there are countless examples of those who have gained and held control of successful business empires by giving their word lightly and breaking it when it suited them. History is full of those who have contrived to cheat their associates, practise deception and manipulate others in order to gain their positions and wealth.

These "dishonourable" CEOs rely, in general, on the existence of people in the world who abide by "honest" principles. In this respect, the morality of honour is very important to the successful CEO even though it is not necessarily part of his own behaviour!

A successful CEO needs to understand that there are only two ways of achieving one's political or corporate objectives, i.e. either according to the rules of so called "fair play" or by recourse to coercion, manipulation, or some other form of political method of control.

Most of us feel that it is more acceptable to abide by the accepted rules of honour but in reality it is often necessary to employ less moral methods to achieve one's objectives.

A successful CEO knows when to be honourable and when to be businesslike.

Honour versus Objectives: how to be pragmatic

A successful chief executive understands how to take a balanced view of both these standards of behaviour according to the circumstances which prevail at any particular moment.

So what are the rules of honour for a CEO?

A prudent chief executive cannot, and must not, honour his word when it places him at a disadvantage, or when, in his opinion, the reasons for making the original promise cease to exist.

If everyone in the world was honest and upright this would be an invalid and immoral statement. However, most people are rarely honourable all the time, rather circumstances play a key role in its use and absence. The issue of circumstance is an essential premise for a chief executive who intends to get his own way. If circumstances allow for a CEO to be honourable then he should be honourable. But if not, then a CEO should not hesitate to do and say anything that is necessary to promote his interests without any hang-ups on the subject of honour.

This isn't such a difficult regime to implement as at first glance it appears to be. No chief executive has ever lacked a good excuse to justify or at least blur his reasons for dishonouring a promise. If he hasn't got a reason, he can simply invent one.

A successful chief executive must be capable of careful deception when it is necessary.

Take the case of Board Metallic Products Ltd., a large engineering company, established in the last century and apparently with some of the original pressing equipment still in use. The old managing director liked a quiet life and had established a good "liberal" relationship with his employees and he meant to keep it that way.

The company had experienced very few industrial relations problems in the past, mainly because it wasn't unionized until recent years. However, after an unfortunate series of accidents, a union was formed and within a short time had become as militant a trade-organisation as was to be found in the industry. Demarcation, wages, holidays, working-conditions, health and safety, productivity all soon became the subjects of daily controversy. But despite these changes, the managing director generally took a conciliatory attitude.

The shop steward was a militant individual who had come to the company from a more up-to-date factory and was not impressed by the pliability and easy going attitude of his "brothers" regarding their rights.

When an economic recession hit the company, (as it did the whole industry), the managing director found himself in a dilemma. He didn't want to stir up trouble and damage his popularity with the management but he did have to increase productivity. This meant new computerized machines, requiring fewer men to operate them, a totally new set of skills, retraining, and perhaps even redundancies. A minefield of changes in organisation, job descriptions and productivity issues lay ahead, and the managing director knew it.

After much soul-searching the chief executive came up with a solution. He waited for another serious accident to happen and then anonymously reported his own company to the Department of Industry's Health and Safety Executive. He provided them with detailed descriptions of all the safety flaws in his (obsolete) equipment.

Within a week the plant was closed by the inspectorate and the employees laid off.

At a meeting of the workers a week later, the managing director expressed his "sincere regrets" about the situation and explained that someone in the plant had reported in some detail, on the large numbers of safety problems. Much of the equipment would have to be replaced during which time the plant would be closed. He assured the workers that the closure would last no more than a month, unfortunately without pay. When the plant was reopened and the new equipment came into service, the CEO offered to rehire employees as and when the need arose.

The managing director started immediately with the refurbishment of the plant with the new computerized machinery and within weeks he was recalling the workers to the plant. As he expected there was no discussion about demarcation, retraining, extra productivity or a few missing colleagues. The workers were glad to be back on the payroll again and they knew that the managing director had been forced to replace the old equipment and was "doing his best for the company".

On the other hand, general suspicion for reporting the company fell squarely on the head of the militant "safety conscious" shop-steward. Union membership cancellations started arriving at once. The general consensus amongst the workforce was that the CEO was justified in not rehiring the militant shop-steward. All in all a very satisfactory result for the chief executive and his company. The company survived the recession, as did the CEO's image as a fatherly and liberal old gentleman.

The image of the "honourable" CEO

However, it is necessary to emphasize again that a chief executive must appear to honour his word, without, of course, doing so when it would be imprudent. The CEO should appear to his employees and associates to be compassionate, faithful, honourable, humane, straight-forward and understanding. Indeed, when it is possible he should be all these. But when it is necessary to act otherwise for the good of the company and the security of his position, he should be capable of ignoring these virtues and act dishonourably.

In the case of a new chief executive, a flexible attitude towards standards of honour is essential. He mustn't give the impression to anyone that he is amoral since it is what he appears to be, rather than what he is and does, that is important. Few people will have sufficiently close contact with him to know his real attitudes and will simply experience his "packaged public image"; the packaging being more important to most people than the contents! The strength of his corporate regime will lend respectability to his actions and discredit any dissenters. When there is no recourse to appeal, then most men tend to judge others by their results and appearances. Few people bother to investigate any further.

---oOo---

20. Avoiding hatred and contempt

I have already briefly touched on this subject in previous chapters but it is sufficiently important to deserve further discussion.

To be avoided

A chief executive should avoid any action which will result in his being hated or despised. Provided that he is not violently disliked by his employees, he will always be forgiven for any other flaws in his personality or unpopular actions. So long as he doesn't interfere with the primary needs of his employees (or the majority of them), they will remain reasonably content. He has then only to contend with the ambitions of the few, and these can be dealt with easily and in several ways.

What attracts the contempt of others?

The qualities which really attract contempt to a chief executive are inconsistency, frivolity, cowardice and indecision. A chief executive should always try to manage with an air of grandeur, courage and strength. His directives must always be irrevocable and non-negotiable, and he must always give the impression that it is impossible to deceive or circumvent him. A chief executive who achieves this degree of esteem will appear difficult to conspire against and will attract less opposition from inside or outside his organisation. It is crucial to the maintenance of his position.

Why is it important?

If the chief executive develops his management style in this way he need not fear any opposition and he will inspire the respect and achieve the contentment of his workforce. If he doesn't have the workforce with him he will find it hard to weather any storms which might blow the company's way because there will be too many employees who don't take him seriously, dislike him or don't trust him.

All corporate predators know that they will be successful, if, by hurting or removing the chief executive, they will satisfy the company's employees. Similarly they know that they will fail if they outrage the company's employees. A company is therefore much more secure if it has a contented and faithful workforce that respects its CEO.

The importance of having the respect of the workforce

In the case of a conspiracy to take over a company or oust its chief executive, there must be several persons working together, and these, in some way, must be disgruntled and harbour resentment towards the current management.

But whilst the conspirators are envious and ambitious, they are also fearful of failure and its consequences. The chief executive has a status, his own resources and legal recourse on his side. Allied with the goodwill and support of most of his employees it is unthinkable for anyone to consider attempting to remove him. Not only before but also after such an attempt, those who conspire against the management are in danger, especially if the management has a supportive workforce. When a chief executive has the support of his employees he need not be so concerned about conspiracies against him.

On the other hand, when a CEO's employees are hostile and he is disliked and despised, he must constantly be on his guard because literally everyone is conspiring against him at some level.

Maintaining contentment amongst the workforce, placidity and loyalty amongst the management team is of primary importance to the successful CEO.

Take, for example, Pirus Computer Systems Ltd[19.1], a fast growing software house, wholly owned by a sleeping partner and run by a young managing director whom he appointed. The managing director was promised an equity stake dependent upon the company's performance under his management.

The young managing director easily met and surpassed the set sales targets, albeit in his own unconventional way. He was well-respected and liked by all his employees and customers but his methods antagonized the owner who felt threatened by the managing director's superior ability. He feared that he was losing control of the company.

The company's turnover continued to soar ahead with some spectacular successes and gradually the managing director became less tolerant of the complaints and conservatism of the owner. Simultaneously, the owner seemed to be dragging his feet on the issue of equity-distribution to the young managing director.

Eventually, at a particularly busy time, the owner interfered in a sale and there was a major showdown between the owner and managing director. All the contentious issues came out and the managing director unconditionally resigned. He was immediately replaced by one of the owner's friends.

Six weeks later the company was effectively ruined. The managing director had started his own company in the same business. He stripped the best employees from the old operation, contacted old customers and established an instant business-base, much to the detriment of the old company.

Employee perceptions of moral behaviour

In this example the owner of the company ignored an important principle of successful management, namely that a prudent chief executive should always be personally responsible for the awarding of benefits, but should delegate the implementation of unpopular directives as much as possible to others. In this case, the managing director was seen as the saviour of the employees' jobs and the owner of the company was painted as the "wrecker" of the company. In these circumstances it was easy for the young CEO to get the upper hand.

Finally, a prudent chief executive should also remember that he can just as easily be hated for the good things he does as for the bad. This is because at the end of the day most people are only interested in what benefits them, avoiding anything which would harm them, and are not much interested, unless they have to be, in what happens to other employees.

A chief executive who is striving to maintain control must therefore be realistic. Those who help him to maintain his status and position, shareholders, co-directors, managers and workers, are inherently amoral. In such an environment, the chief executive may also be forced to set aside his morality - simply in order to survive.

---o0o---

21. The value of management expedients

Types of expedient

To maintain control of a company a chief executive often employs certain manipulative contrivances against his employees. The CEO may minimize the amount of power given to various employees or weaken workers' solidarity by dividing groups of workers into conflicting groups, deliberately fostering animosity between disruptive elements within the company. He might infiltrate potentially troublesome factions. All the while, however, the CEO appears to employ a policy of open management to avoid employee distrust[20.1].

Are these expedients useful?

It is impossible to pinpoint the value of any particular expedient without first examining the circumstances in which it is used, so here I will only discuss them in general.

Granting employee responsibility

Rarely should a new chief executive openly curtail the power of his employees, rather, he should appear to be providing them with greater responsibility. The logic is this will attract the loyalty of those who are antagonistic towards him whilst increasing the dedication of those already loyal to him.

Since it is impossible for everyone to be given greater responsibility, the chief executive must be selective as to whom he gives more power. This promotion will create an obligation for those who are promoted but will soon be forgotten and forgiven by those who are overlooked.

This latter group will come to believe that their promoted colleagues run a greater risk of failure than they do. They will even come to believe that were lucky not to be promoted and were in fact treated favourably by the CEO. The perception is that the bigger you are, the harder you fall.

Withdrawing employee responsibility

One can never successfully take away power from an employee once it has been given. If it is necessary to reduce the power of a staff member, one must actually remove him or her. Dismissal is the only way.

Once an employee's power is curtailed, he or she feels offended; no one likes to be regarded as incompetent. Compounding the personal upset is the fact that the offence is public, the affected worker feels he has suffered public humiliation. Even though the CEO had no intention of inflicting these emotional wounds this is how his actions will be perceived by those affected.

In this case hatred and resentment for the chief executive is engendered, and the chief executive may be forced to employ outside assistance such as management consultants to assist him in removing the disgruntled employee(s). The dangers inherent in this recourse have already been discussed. A much better solution is to remove the employee(s) completely before reaching this kind of impasse.

In conclusion, it is generally a good thing for a chief executive to extend and increase the power of his managers and the responsibilities of the workforce.

The exception to this is when a chief executive takes control of another company. As I have already said, it is essential that the chief executive removes or severely restricts the power of the old managers until he knows their attitude towards him. He should transfer their power to his own personnel or promote other potentially useful personnel within the company who are not a threat to him. Ultimately, if these managers are not to be trusted they have to be completely removed.

Divide and rule: If and when this is useful

It is often argued that it is better to rule by dividing one's subordinates rather than by uniting them. This technique of control is quite feasible and may be useful in some circumstances, it is often necessary in stable times.

However, in difficult periods this expedient is much less useful and indeed can be counter-productive. In troublesome times the chief executive needs all the help he can get. He shouldn't be dividing his employees to pre-empt any attack on him, rather he should be galvanizing them to help in the defence of the company.

Indeed, rare is the case where the technique of "divide and rule" is actually useful. It is generally counter-productive to the chief executive's primary objectives of security and profit. It wastes and saps a lot of the employees' energy in a totally non-productive way. Frequently it signals weakness or a lack of imagination on the part of the chief executive. When unity is called for, as in times of difficulty, the use of this expedient can be disastrous.

The only occasional use and value of the "divide and rule" expedient is when a company is operating in stable conditions and under no threat. Here it has a limited value in destabilizing internal cliques which the chief executive feels may be a threat to him.

Creating artificial disputes

Another hybrid of the above technique is the deliberate fostering of dissention and disunity in order that the chief executive may improve his own status by subsequently intervening and settling the dispute.

An imaginative CEO may even foster disaffection towards himself and then proceed to root out the ringleaders and sympathizers (whom he originally targeted for dismissal). His actions will be seen as wholly justified by the rest of the workforce and the troublemakers will have been removed without too much fuss or opposition.

Playing "Open Management"

Let us now turn to the policy of open management. This is a most commendable ploy with many rewarding fringe benefits. One important side effect is a better understanding between staff and the CEO. By appearing to operate an open management system, a great deal of information emerges about the attitudes of the management team and workforce concerning the company and its chief executive.

Ironically, many chief executives often find that staff members initially antagonistic at the start of the CEO's tenure, gradually turn out to be more loyal and useful employees than those who immediately profess their loyalty and cooperation. This has a lot to do with the real motivation of the employee who may be supportive of the company whilst initially opposing the new CEO. Open management can reveal such anachronisms.

For example, when Transtec Ltd., a data processing agency, was bought and managed by an outside businessman, he was met with a mixture of hostility, apathy, and cooperation amongst the employees[20.2].

He found that the apathetic employee continued to be indifferent towards him and their work. The cooperative workers became intolerably ingratiating and were obviously mainly interested in keeping their jobs and protecting their own interests. The really antagonistic continued to be outspoken.

When the company ran into financial troubles some months after the take-over, the managing director called for the assistance and cooperation of everyone in the company to help see the company through its troubles. This meant extra unpaid hours, cancelled holidays and so on. The reactions to the CEO's calls were not what he had expected.

Those employees who were "cooperative" suddenly became preoccupied with their own survival and continuously complained of the detrimental impact of the measures on them personally. They found many excuses to avoid any form of inconvenient personal commitments to the company. However, the antagonists became staunch supporters of the measures, they were still outspoken but were productive in their comments and defensive about the company. The apathetic continued as always, indifferent.

In general, a chief executive will never have difficulty gaining solid support from those who were initially openly opposed to him, once they begin to trust the CEO and become dependent upon him. They will be all the more loyal in their service to him because they will feel obliged to make up for their initial distrust. These employees who were once openly hostile towards the CEO, were bold enough to voice their antagonistic feelings. Having swung their weight behind the CEO, they will also be brave in his defence. They will certainly be much more loyal and dedicated than those employees who had only given lip service to the chief executive in the past in order to survive by not "rocking the boat".

The essence of an open management system is to create the impression that a company is liberal, and that its liberality must be respected and not abused. This translates into keeping the workforce pliant and communicative. It also precludes most types of industrial dispute because everyone will see an offensive launched against such a liberal minded chief executive as an outrage.

If the chief executive is reporting either to a board of directors over whom he has no control or to other shareholders, then the policy of open management will allow him to relocate blame for any decision which backfires. The decision will have been an apparently joint decision of the management team, not just his own. This is an excellent way of deflecting and diluting blame when necessary.

Controlling openness in management

When a chief executive wants to be tough he can always close the ranks of management and thus reduce the degree of real participation and openness that he permits. So we see that the degree of management openness he allows is a function of circumstances.

Advantages of "Open management"

Openness in management only works if the chief executive has the cooperation and support of his management and workforce. With this backing open management is feasible and an excellent mechanism for maintaining harmony between the management and workforce.

Open management is one of the best defences the chief executive has against employee animosity.

---o0o---

22. Gaining prestige

Why does a CEO need prestige and how does he achieve it?

Clearly a successful CEO wishes and needs to be respected. To do this he needs to garner prestige. Nothing attracts prestige to a chief executive more than successful corporate campaigns of various kinds and striking demonstrations of his personal ability. Let me illustrate this point with an example.

Kastroflex Ltd., an electrical goods producer, was a long established and conservatively managed enterprise[21.1]. The employees were generally disinterested in their work or the company and uninspired by its management. The high points of their year were the annual pay negotiations and the Christmas party. When a new chief executive was appointed, the board and shareholders were astounded and disconcerted by the radical change in behaviour of both the workforce and the management. Both morale and, more importantly, productivity improved almost at once. What had changed?

The new chief executive was not a particularly astute businessman or able engineer but he exuded strength of will and was seen as adventurous and likeable. He appeared to be totally in control, dynamic, serious and concerned. And yet when his actions were analyzed, there didn't seem to be anything concrete to which his success could be attributed. Sales continued at much the same level as before his arrival, but profits improved significantly.

When his first year as chief executive was over, he had basically just moved the production-lines around, installed some small labour-saving equipment and re-equipped the canteen. No great achievements there, one might think, but it was his manner of instituting change which was significant. He did everything with great panache and was a great self-publicist.

This CEO was a tremendous motivator and made a point of addressing all the employees once a week to report on the company's performance related to his projected targets. He was an absolute master of bravado, and everything he did was done with tremendous ceremony. He never failed to broadcast the details of the company's successes and he announced his small initiatives as if they were revolutionary. In other words, his mediocre business sense was more than compensated for by his ability to engage with his employees and customers alike. Their respect and confidence in him as a likeable and natural leader was universal.

Decisiveness

A chief executive also gains prestige by demonstrating decisiveness in times of difficulty. This personal quality is certainly more advantageous to the CEO than being too cautious. This is because a wise decision had a good chance of success whilst even a weaker one may still succeed. But in the event where the CEO makes no decision, the company is almost certainly doomed: it becomes a rudderless firm helplessly tossed towards the unforgiving rocks of corporate failure.

This principle is equally valid when it comes to taking sides in any kind of dispute, both internal and external. Decisiveness is essential. Let's take an example:

In Trendco Ltd[21.2] a young executive developed a marketing plan for a new product. His plan was somewhat radical and it immediately became a contentious issue amongst the other managers. Some took his side, claiming that his strategy was fresh and innovative. Others saw the plans as naive and dangerous. A dispute developed.

The chief executive soon became aware that the dispute was becoming serious and was needlessly preoccupying his management team. He knew he would have to resolve the dispute and make a decision one way or another although several of his managers, including the young executive's superior, suggested that it would all blow over and he "shouldn't interfere in these things". But he did.

The CEO reviewed and adopted the new marketing plan and made the young executive responsible for its success by giving him his boss's job. He also surveyed the views of all the other members of the management team. Opinions were mixed; some held strong and vocal positions whereas others were indifferent. Some pretended to be non-committal and hid their real opinions from the CEO for fear of retribution.

The CEO then began to root out the uncommitted managers from his management team, suggesting that the individuals resign from the company. Finally, the CEO called a meeting of all employees.

It was a fait accompli. At this meeting he announced the full scale of resignations and promotions including the promotion of the young executive who had triggered off the dispute.

Remarkably, within a week the whole dispute simply dissolved in the wake of this strength of action. Indeed, several weeks later it had already been totally forgotten by the staff when the chief executive expressed his gratitude to those who had felt so strongly about the company's interests as to become personally involved.

The CEO recognised that the disinterested managers were more of a threat to the company than those who argued passionately for a particular course of action. His decisiveness in dealing with the issue brought him a lot of prestige and a reputation as a strong and fair-minded boss.

Beware of indecision

A prudent chief executive will soon realise that whoever urges him to be neutral or indecisive is not acting in the best interests of the company or the chief executive. At least those who urge him to act in one way or another are themselves resolute, decisive and interested.

Those who follow the path of inaction do so because they are afraid of the consequences of an incorrect decision. These types of people inevitably come to grief in the end as they have ceased to be the masters of their own destiny. A company with a weak and indecisive captain will inevitably founder.

Choose your allies carefully

In order to maintain his prestige a chief executive should never ally himself or his company to any person or entity more powerful than he himself. If he does and the relationship is initially successful, he and his company become subject to the influence of his ally.

If the relationship is not successful, then the CEO will be under threat from the old ally and will be dependent upon their goodwill to some extent. A wise chief executive should always avoid any form of dependence for several reasons, not least because he must always protect against any possible damage to his prestige.

Facing up to problems

A chief executive should never imagine for one moment that avoiding a problem will allow him to escape it. So often in the flight from one dangerous situation, the unwise chief executive jumps from the frying pan into the fire.

All courses of action contain some element of risk. Prudence is the ability to select the optimal course of action. It does not lie in being indecisive or in ignoring problems.

Generosity - rewarding talent and ability

A chief executive should always reward the talent and ability of his employees and he should promote those who are faithful to his regime. This involves providing a ready means of promotion and security of employment to those who are dedicated and work with the good of the company and its chief executive as their primary goals.

The wise chief executive should provide other rewards to his employees too, such as social events etc. which serve the important role of unifying and gratifying the staff. He should go out of his way to meet and entertain workers' representatives on a regular basis whilst at all times maintaining the dignity of his position.

Gaining prestige is not just a matter of being obviously successful, it is also the art of appearing magnanimous, open-minded and liberal.

---oOo---

23. The chief executive's inner circle

Importance of the management team

The most important action of a chief executive is the selection of his management team. It is probably also one of the hardest tasks which he will ever have to undertake because the value of those he selects depends entirely upon his ability to judge the character of a candidate.

You can always judge a chief executive's ability by looking at the quality of the managers he has hired. When his managers are competent and loyal he is considered prudent and perceptive about people. When his managers demonstrate less ability and faithfulness the CEO's judgement is also discredited.

This is because the CEO has compounded his initial error, not only did he hire a manager of inferior ability but his failure to recognise that or do anything about it has made him doubly culpable in the eyes of those surrounding him. The chief executive is roundly condemned as a fool.

Choosing managers

In terms of management ability there are three types of personality which the chief executive will encounter:

- -Those individuals who understand management instinctively

- Those capable of learning how to manage well

- Those that do not understand good management and cannot be taught

The first type is excellent, the second good, the third useless. If one cannot have managers of the first type, then the second is acceptable. The third must be avoided at all costs. This statement may seem obvious but it is amazing how many managers are hired on the basis of their contacts or on the basis of paper qualifications rather than on the basis of their demonstrable talent for management.

Motivation and personnel selection

So much has been written on the subject of personnel selection and it is such a subjective topic that I believe it would be unwise to dwell on the subject here. All a chief executive really has to do when recruiting a manager is to keep clear in his mind what basic personal characteristics he finds essential and what other traits he considers desirable. After that it is simply a matter of working through candidates and not compromising on these requirements.

There is one infallible rule of thumb which should always be applied by a chief executive when he is assessing potential managers. Neither a candidate who considers himself and his own interests above those of the company or the chief executive, nor an applicant who is opinionated and inflexible will ever be satisfactory. These types of individual can never be trusted or trained.

It is far better to hire an eager, trustworthy person who can be "developed" and trained, even though he may not have all the necessary experience or academic qualifications. An ambitious, self-centred and selfish individual, albeit with apparently better qualifications and experience, is often not to be trusted.

Qualifications and experience in a manager are not everything. A person to be entrusted with assisting the management of a company must consider nothing but the good of the company and the chief executive. Everything else must be subordinated to this loyalty.

Flexibility and personnel selection

The managers that a chief executive hires must be flexible, especially when it comes to solving problems and exploiting opportunities. They must be imaginative but also capable of controlling and channelling this imagination into constructive activities. Such people do exist and a wise chief executive should always hold out until he finds the right management personnel.

How to manage the managers

A chief executive should always be considerate to the managers he finally appoints. He should unstintingly confer all the appropriate remuneration, status, responsibility and recognition upon them.

At the same time a chief executive should also engender their dependence upon him and the company. In a nutshell, he must ask a lot of his managers but he must also reward them well, and not just financially.

Conversely, a chief executive should always demand and exercise strict discipline over his management team. He must demand honesty and obedience, and the penalty for not getting these should be made clear to them.

By doing this, his managers will soon recognize their dependence, and, if properly rewarded, will not require further motivation. Only when this type of relationship is established will a manager respect his chief executive and can the chief executive trust his manager.

---oOo---

24. Dealing with deception

Types of deception

An important issue which all chief executives must confront at some stage is deception, either by others, or self-deception induced by others out of self-interest.

There are always managers who will try to flatter and ingratiate themselves with the chief executive to deceive him in some way. It is difficult not to become a victim of this phenomenon because there are sycophantic personalities in all walks of life, highly credible, who are pursuing their own agendas.

Dealing with deception

It is not enough to simply pretend that such people do not exist in an organisation and hope for the best, this doesn't resolve anything! A wise chief executive must never shy away from an unresolved problem in that way. Ideally, the chief executive would select the right managers in the first place, eliminating those in the organisation who are deceitful or insincere but this is with the benefit of hindsight, somewhat retrospective advice!

Approachability

It is very important that a chief executive encourages his managers to be candid with him. He must make it quite clear to all of his managers that he is neither afraid nor offended by the truth. He must also avoid being or appearing tyrannical because this will make him unapproachable, and a dictatorial chief executive will always attract or create a sycophantic management team.

A chief executive must encourage honesty and be approachable; however, I would add one word of caution. A chief executive must be careful that his managers do not abuse their right of access to him. He must not permit gratuitous advice.

Taking and implementing advice

The CEO must implement a proper procedure for receiving advice from his management team. The procedure he should adopt should involve some kind of regular reporting and communicating mechanism. When the CEO is particularly interested in hearing someone's opinion he will canvass it directly. The chief executive should then question these opinions, listen carefully to what is recommended, and only then make up his own mind, alone.

The CEO must induce a feeling within the management team that the more plainly they speak, the more credit he will give them. Advice, other than from those he has selected to join his management team, should be disregarded and unsolicited suggestions should be discouraged and viewed with suspicion. A chief executive should implement his conclusions at once and adhere rigidly to his plans.

Any chief executive who does not observe these rules will always be subject to deception and manipulation. He will become hesitant, his decisions irresolute and finally the CEO will lose the esteem of his managers and workforce.

Failure to listen to advice

Any chief executive, who is very secretive, refuses to take advice, discuss policy or involve his management in formulating his plans and making decisions, may think that he is maintaining his elitist position and thereby affirming his authority, but he is not. In fact this attitude has the opposite effect.

What happens in these circumstances is that when the chief executive attempts to implement any operational changes, he is met with extraordinary resistance. His plans generally end in failure. Even if he does manage to implement a plan, it never stands up for long.

This is because none of the CEO's staff feel that they are involved in the conception, development, or implementation of such a plan. It appears to be a completely alien idea that is being imposed upon them from above. It is most important therefore that all employees, including managers, are made to feel that they have contributed to a plan if they are to "buy into" the idea and make it work. Their real contribution may be negligible but this is not important. What they perceive as their contribution may well be more important than the contribution itself.

A secretive and uncommunicative chief executive will continuously be taking action and springing plans on a surprised workforce with no input or contribution from anyone else in the company. These proposals will consequently be resented and resisted[23.1].

The wisdom of listening to the advice of others

A chief executive shouldn't consider it a weakness to seek and take advice from others, provided, as I have said, that he only does so when he himself asks for it, and not when others seek to proffer it. I reiterate, a wise CEO must discourage unsolicited advice.

A chief executive should be a constant questioner of his employees, listening patiently and attentively to them even if he already knows what they are telling him. If he detects that anyone is withholding the truth or trying to deceive him, he must take severe disciplinary action against that person.

Whose advice?

A chief executive cannot be well advised unless he is shrewd enough to distinguish good advice from bad. If he relies entirely on the advice of his managers, the chief executive becomes irrelevant to the organisation and cannot maintain his position. He should be capable of enlisting and hearing suggestions from his lowliest employee to his most senior specialist.

One criterion for judging a chief executive is his ability and instinct to recognize and accept good advice. The ability of a chief executive is not solely dependent on the quality of the advice he is given, but on his ability to distinguish good advice from bad.

---oOo---

25. Why some chief executives lose their companies

New CEOs

If all the rules enunciated above are adhered to a new chief executive will quickly become a solid, well-established and successful leader and will soon consolidate his position in the company as its natural head.

A new chief executive will attract more attention than a long-established CEO and if his behaviour is inspiring and courageous, he will soon overcome suspicion and dissent. If he hires effective and dedicated managers and treats his employees and management team well, he will soon come to be seen as reasonable and liberal and will gradually make firm, long-lasting allegiances amongst his personnel.

If there has been some unpleasantness before, during and immediately after his arrival this will soon be forgotten if he is consistent. This is because people tend to be more concerned with the present than with the past. If they are happy with their current situation, they will soon forget past problems and will be content.

What can go wrong?

Why is it then that so many chief executives lose control of their companies or lose their position? Why is there such a turnover in these top jobs?

If we consider those chief executives who have lost control of their companies, we can observe many common factors.

Ill-prepared

One reason for a chief executive's failure is a lack of preparation for dealing with adverse situations, whether they be financial, personnel or operational. As I have said, there is little point in starting to make plans to deal with an emergency when it has already arrived. There must be contingency plans ready to put into operation at short notice.

Bad blood, resentment and dependency

Another common reason for failure is that a chief executive may have incurred, for whatever reason, the hatred of his workforce or disrespect of his management. In these circumstances he cannot survive. Finally, a growing dependence upon others is frequently observed shortly before a collapse.

Survival summary, flaws to watch out for

No company can survive if these issues are not properly addressed. Those who fail to provide for troubled times are commonly complacent, self-deceptive and indecisive. Those who alienate their personnel are usually short-sighted egotists. The chief executive who allows himself to become dependent is weak, naive or both.

Business is a hard master, demanding constant vigilance, an extraordinary range of talents and an instinct for survival well in excess of that required in everyday life[24.1].

---oOo---

26. Opportunism versus ability

The mythology of "fate" in business

Most people, including many chief executives, believe that there are certain events outside their control and over which they have absolutely no influence. Consequently, they are fatalistic. Many rational business people readily submit themselves stoically to any chance event if they can't see any immediate way in which they can influence or exploit the events unfolding around them.

The competent opportunist: the ideal CEO

However, in reality whilst we cannot foresee the future in detail, we can, as every true opportunist knows, construct realistic scenarios about the future and be prepared for what may be in store for us, whether it be auspicious or ill-omened, and turn these events to our advantage.

We can make provisional plans, manage our risks scientifically and take precautions. It is this combination of a chief executive's foresight with real management ability which he must strive to develop in himself. In other words, he should seek to display the instinct of the opportunist and the circumspection of the able manager.

For example, if CEOs in the Western industrial nations had paid more attention to events in the Far East over the last forty years and had, instead of remaining complacent, started planning and investing to deal with the external competition in its embryonic stage, our traditional markets would not now overwhelmed by foreign competitors with better, cheaper products. We could have stemmed the tsunami with just a little more foresight and a lot less insularity and "hoping for the best" [25.1] - wishful optimism.

Flexibility is the key

The keyword in effective management is flexibility, the ability to adapt quickly to the needs of the times. The individual who adopts a set of rigid policies and codes of practice doesn't survive.

The methods used by any chief executive may only be judged by his ability to achieve corporate and personal objectives. The achievement of prosperity is ephemeral, and whilst circumspection and patience may be appropriate today, they may be irrelevant tomorrow.

Let us take two individuals with similar backgrounds and personalities, for instance they are both cautious. Why it is that one might succeed completely in his ambitions whilst the other may fail spectacularly? It is because different fields of industry require different human characteristics. Let us elaborate.

Be bold

Some industries, such as the marketing sector, demand adventurous management whilst others, such as the legal profession, require a more measured approach. The entertainment and computer industry is full of "hype", the textile industry a lot more traditional.

What is important is the ability of the CEO to adapt his management strategy to the industry and circumstances in which he is operating[25.2]. Markets and manufacturing methods change so quickly these days that any CEO standing still is actually going backwards in relation to his competitors. He will soon slip below the horizon to be forgotten.

In general, if one must make a choice between being circumspect and impetuous, then it is better to be impulsive. In this way the subject may at least learn from his actions. When a CEO is too conservative, he will probably learn nothing, so "be bold" is the watchword of the good chief executive.

---oOo---

27. A final word of encouragement to the aspiring chief executive

After all these deliberations I wonder if the time is yet right for the emergence of the ideal chief executive I have described, especially in the face of the liberalization of the profit motive and the decline of strong management in Western commerce

I suppose it is necessary and natural for industry and commerce to have periods of lacklustre management in order that opportunities be available for the next generation of inspired entrepreneurial chief executives.

Certainly, faced with such poverty of executive management ability, if ever there was a time when a chief executive embodying the qualities I have described was needed, then it is now.

Our industrial and commercial enterprises are leaderless, lawless, uninspired, demoralised and largely controlled by foreign capital. Industry cries out for leadership and prowess.

It will not be an easy task to reverse this situation but opportunities abound for those who are willing to seize and maintain management control.

As for our ability, the history of western capitalism is full of examples of our management capability, although now sadly dissipated by division and liberality.

As for our workers, there are no better trained and capable of discipline than they. Sadly though, their ranks are now riddled with the agents of self-interest and liberalism, this must be dealt with in order to return our businesses to their previous fortunate positions of world dominance.

But there are also great opportunities for truly talented business leaders and these must not be missed, so I entreat those of you who are reading this to grasp this chance and return the art of executive management to its rightfully respected place amongst the great skills of leadership.

It is impossible to say how greatly a new generation of strong chief executives would now be welcomed, with what loyalty and devotion they would be supported, and the fervour with which workers and management alike would strive to remove the present malignant incompetence, liberalism and inundation by foreign goods and capital!

---oOo---

Notes from "The Prince"

3.1 When Greece was invaded by Turkey in the fifteenth century, the Turks took the wise precaution of settling their new territories and governing them in person, so to speak. The antagonism of the Greeks was so great (and still is), that the Turks could never otherwise have held onto their conquests.

3.2 Machiavelli is very firm on the wisest policy for dealing with powerful elements in a newly conquered territory. They must be totally eliminated if they are at all capable of harming the new ruler. Any compromise invites retaliation against the invaders for any minor grievance. He refers to the Romans who after seizing a country, would crush the incumbent local nationalist leaders and replace them with their own vice-consuls, never permitting any "foreigner" to win or hold honours in Rome itself.

5.1 This example is based on Machiavelli's description of the policy of the Romans in Carthage, Numantia and Greece. For the first two countries, Rome realized it couldn't maintain control of the population and thus demolished the countries' cities, killing and brutalizing many of their citizens in the process However, the Romans thought it was possible for the Greeks to govern themselves as the Spartans had, but this turned out not to be the case. Eventually the Romans razed most of the cities of Greece to the ground to retain their rule.

6.1 Machiavelli's examples of those who gained power by ability rather than just opportunism are somewhat grander than those I have substituted. He cites Moses, Romulus, Theseus, and Cyrus. Further in his discussion on the necessity of adversity, he cites the servitude of the Israelites in Egypt as being Moses' opportunity to become their leader. He feels that Romulus wouldn't have become founder and King of Rome if he hadn't been left in the wilderness to die when he was a baby because he would have missed the chance of being suckled by the famous wolf. More reasonably, Cyrus took advantage of the dissipated state of the Medes and the rebellious attitude of their Persian subjects to seize power.

6.2 Machiavelli makes reference here to Fra Savonarola, one of his contemporaries in the Florentine Republic. Savonarola was a

Dominican monk who despite an inauspicious beginning, rapidly rose in influence and power, he was responsible for the construction of the republic's constitution and largely dominated the republic. He was apparently a captivating orator and his prophetic preaching brought him a fanatical following of both supporters and enemies. His open opposition to the church eventually brought him excommunication. The tide of popular support began to turn against him and he was eventually imprisoned, tortured and executed.

7.1 In this example Machiavelli discusses the relative merits of Francesco Sforza and Cesare Borgia. Sforza, a private citizen using his own ability and means, rose to become Duke of Milan after a great deal of effort. However, he managed to maintain his rule with apparent ease. Cesare Borgia, the son of Cardinal Rodrigo Borgia (later Pope Alexandre VI) and his mistress, was himself created a cardinal by his father, though not a priest. With his born advantage and contacts Borgia soon managed to become Duke of Valence and Duke of Romagna. These are for Machiavelli, prime examples of real ability in Sforza and opportunism in Borgia. Machiavelli is more impressed by ability but holds that opportunism is also an essential personal characteristic.

7.2 One of the more gruesome exploits of Cesare Borgia was his strategy of governing the Romagna. The state had been weakly ruled for some time and was in a condition of near anarchy. Borgia gave wide-ranging powers to Remirro de Orco, a cruel though apparently efficient man, to bring the Romagna into line. When the Romagna had been subdued Borgia set up a civil tribunal and gave each city a representative. Knowing that he was hated by the population, Borgia went to lengths to alter this public perception. He contrived to create the impression that the cruelty the citizens had endured was the responsibility of his minister and not that of their prince personally. Once established, this gave Cesare the necessary pretext to enact the next part of his plan. One morning the body of de Orco was found cut into two pieces in a piazza next to a butcher's wooden block and knife. This kept the people of the Romagna happy, though a little puzzled, for some time. This outrageous act of brutality left a deep impression on Machiavelli who was a virtual eye-witness to it. Whilst he was shocked by its brutality, he was impressed by Borgia's planning, resolve, swiftness of action and the economy with which he exercised what he believed to be necessary cruelty.

8.1 During the pontificate of Alexandre VI there was a young orphan named Oliverotto of Fermo who was brought up by his uncle. This young man is Machiavelli's example of gaining power by criminal means. Oliverotto was sent to serve and be trained as a soldier under Paulo Vitelli, a mercenary. After Paulo was executed, Oliverotto soldiered under the command of his brother and in a very short time became his brother's commander-in-chief. But he wasn't happy with this servile position and decided to seize Fermo for himself.

Oliverotto wrote to his uncle and asked if he would organize an honourable homecoming for him and his hundred or so mounted servants and guards in order that he might see his home city again. His uncle willingly agreed to throw a reception for him and after a few days he arrived in Fermo where he was treated with a great deal of hospitality. After a few days he requested that the chief personages of the city be invited for dinner at his mansion. Shortly after eating, he requested a private conference with these important citizens. No sooner had they seated themselves than his soldiers, hidden in recesses in the room, emerged and murdered his uncle and the other city fathers. Oliverotto then proceeded to besiege the palace and council. Having rid himself of all those whom he could expect to fear, Oliverotto soon persuaded the council to set up a government with him as its Prince. He consolidated his position by issuing new civil and military instructions.

However, Oliverotto was only in power for just over a year. Tricked by Cesare Borgia, he was found strangled along with his brother whom Machiavelli considered his teacher, both in virtues of princedom and in crime.

9.1 I have compared here the differences in loyalty which Machiavelli observed between Renaissance noblemen and the magistrates and other minor dignitaries of the city-states. He distrusted both the magistrates and the noblemen but felt that the noblemen could at least be controlled by a prince. In my interpretation the shareholders and directors of a company are the noblemen of Machiavelli's world, our corporate managers his magistrates.

11.1 Machiavelli was well-known for his anti-clerical feelings. He devoted an entire tract of "The Prince" to "Ecclesiastical Principalities" and he was not very complementary about their government. Today's civil service is most nearly comparable with the highly-developed infrastructure of the church in Mediaeval and Renaissance Europe. Its authority was absolute, underpinned by the ultimate authority in the person of the pope. The influence of the church extended into virtually every area of life: education, health, real estate. It had its own military force and exacted separate taxes. It was unchallengeable, both by princes and private citizens. In Machiavelli's time the Church continued its policy of amassing wealth and influence as before by initiating "holy wars" and manipulating civil governments.

12.1 In line with Machiavelli's policy that a prince must remain independent, he is adamant that the ideal ruler must organize his own armed forces efficiently. He disapproves firmly of mercenary forces of any kind, and not without just cause. Machiavelli had witnessed one of the most ignominious displays of mercenary and auxiliary betrayal in Florentine history. During Florence's attempt to re-conquer Pisa with the assistance of the French, the Gascon mercenaries deserted during the siege, and the Swiss auxiliaries mutinied for more pay. The siege of Pisa collapsed and the Florentines were forced to go home having accomplished nothing. The obvious comparison in modern industry is the management consultant, that ever popular cure-all of unimaginative managements. Machiavelli is absolutely scathing in his comments on mercenary and auxiliary troops, referring to them as useless and dangerous. This is not difficult to understand in the context of renaissance Italy, mired in a continuous state of disunity and warfare; it was a ready market for many mercenary and foreign armies. Machiavelli's low regard for their loyalty and prowess as soldiers is amply illustrated by historical fact.

16.1 Machiavelli discusses generosity with regard to the behaviour of Pope Julius II and the kings of France and Spain. Julius gained a reputation for generosity to become pope, but he discontinued this largesse thereafter because he wanted to finance his wars. The kings of France and Spain also managed to wage war and maintain their armies only because they were notoriously parsimonious but still they didn't levy any extra taxes either. Machiavelli considers this preferable to a reputation for generosity.

19.1 In reference to the importance of avoiding contempt and hatred, Machiavelli uses the example of the assassination by the Canneschi of Annibale Bentivolgi, a popular leader of Bologna. His popularity was such that the people rose up and killed the Canneschi. When they discovered that a remote relation of Annibale was living in Florence, albeit the son of a blacksmith, they entrusted the government of Bologna to him until Annibale's own son was old enough to rule the city.

20.1 Discussing expediency in government, Machiavelli refers to the belief of some Italian Princes that it was necessary to control Pistoia by using factions and Pisa by using fortresses. They therefore fostered dissention and internal strife amongst the citizens of certain Italian cities. Machiavelli doesn't really approve of this expedient because he believes it weakens the state in the face of attack from an enemy.

20.2 Regarding the behaviour of a Prince's subjects in times of adversity, Machiavelli cites the case of Pandolfo Petrucci, the ruler of Siena, who managed to govern his state more with the support of those who had originally been antagonistic to him than with those who had initially been cooperative.

21.1 In Machiavelli's time gaining "honour" was very important to a Prince. Today we refer to this desire as seeking prestige amongst our fellows. Machiavelli discusses Ferdinand of Aragon, the King of Spain, whom he considers a new prince because of the weak state of his kingdoms when he gained power. Machiavelli considered Ferdinand a good example of how a leader may gain prestige. During Ferdinand's assault on Granada he managed to keep his Castilean barons so tied up in the war that they couldn't cause any trouble at home. Machiavelli liked this. He also admired Ferdinand for using money from the church to finance the war, consequently he was able to establish an experienced standing army for Spain. Somewhat cynically, Machiavelli also describes Ferdinand's use of the pretext of religion in his expulsion of all Arabs over 14 years from Granada and for his attack on Africa. Machiavelli feels that the grandness of the scale on which Ferdinand operated, (wherever the money came from), brought him both honour amongst his subjects and protection from anyone conspiring against him.

21.2 Machiavelli frowns upon indecision. He quotes from Roman history to demonstrate the folly of neutrality. When the Aetolians invited Antiochus, King of Syria, into Greece to expel the Roman forces, Antiochus sent messengers into Greece to try to persuade the Achaean allies of the Romans, to stand aside. The Romans wanted the Achaeans to fight with them. The matter was finally debated in the council of the Achaeans with both a Roman legate urging a decision and an ambassador of Antiochus urging neutrality. The Roman legate's contention was that "neutrality was the least advisable step of all since non-intervention would only ensure that the neutral side would be the prize of the victor, regardless who it was, and would be so without favour or dignity". Today we would say that impartially causes one to "fall between two stools".

23.1 In terms of taking and accepting advice from others, Machiavelli is quite clear. Ask for advice from those you trust, no one else. When a policy is agreed, implement it rigidly and at once. He discusses the behaviour of Maximilian the Emperor as recounted by Bishop Luca who was in his service. Apparently the Emperor never sought nor took any advice from anyone. He was secretive and neither consulted nor informed his councillors. Consequently, as soon as he put his plans into action they were met with instant opposition. Puzzled over this, he would finally take advice from absolutely anyone. At this point he was easily diverted from his original course of action and his plans usually fell into total disarray. Thus concludes Machiavelli, "What the Emperor achieved one day, was undone the next". His plans and intentions were always unclear and unreliable with his supporters unable to understand what he really wanted.

24.1 There are many examples of princes who have lost their states, but in this section Machiavelli decides to cite one who kept his. Philip of Macedon was the ruler of a minor dominion. He was a military man but he knew how to keep the people content and his noblemen obedient. Despite concerted attacks by the mighty Romans with their Greek auxiliaries, he kept up a war against them for many years, and despite some losses, held onto his kingdom. Machiavelli makes some scathing comments against Italian rulers but he doesn't mention them by name or gives any examples of their ineptitude, weakness or incompetence. This would not have been a wise thing to do in Machiavelli's position!

25.1 Machiavelli was preoccupied with the need to make adequate military provisions against any potential enemy in time of peace. He admires the Germans, French and Spanish who spent vast sums on building fortresses and training their subjects in the art of warfare. Italy, he bemoans, did none of this, and he sees this as one of the major causes of its domination by foreigners.

25.2 Machiavelli considered Pope Julius II a bold but impetuous leader who was incapable of being circumspect; however his impetuosity was appropriate to the times in which he lived. Machiavelli recalls Julius' campaign against Bologna. His plans were mistrusted by everyone: the Venetians, the Spanish and the French. But Julius launched the campaign anyway and furthermore led it himself. This disconcerted the Spanish and Venetians and brought the French along in the tide of action. Certainly Julius would not have succeeded if he had acted more prudently. His allies would have found plenty of reasons for delaying the campaign and it would probably never have taken place. As it was, they were swept along by his audacity. He took them all by surprise, including Bologna.

---oOo---

About the author and editor

Malcolm Coxall, the author, is a management consultant and systems analyst with more than 30 years experience. Starting with a career in industrial dispute arbitration for the International Labour Organisation, Malcolm later became a free-lance systems consultant, working in mainland Europe and the Middle East.

With experience working for many of the world's largest corporate and institutional players, Malcolm has acquired a ringside view of the human, organisational and management methodologies used by medium and large businesses in industries as diverse as banking, oil, defence, telecoms, manufacturing, mining, food, agriculture, aerospace, textiles and engineering.

Malcolm has published articles on sociology, political manipulation, sustainable agriculture, organic food production, forest biodiversity, environmental protection and environmental economics. Malcolm is the author of "Human Manipulation - A Handbook" and a series of textbooks dealing with relational database design ("Oracle Quick Guides"). He is active in European environmental politics and was a successful private complainant in the European Court of Justice in several cases of national breaches of European environmental law. He now lives in southern Spain from where he continues his IT consultancy work and writing, whilst managing the family's organic farm.

Guy Caswell, the editor, was born in Southampton, UK in 1955. He spent his formative years in Nigeria and worked in various jobs in England before leaving for Thailand in 1992, where he divides his time between teaching English in Bangkok and the family farm in the north-east of Thailand.

Guy graduated from Ramkhamhaeng University majoring in Thai language. As an English tutor, Guy claims to have the longest serving student in the world, a prominent Thai politician whom he has tutored continuously for 17 years. Guy's interests include playing the guitar, farming, politics and Thai culture.

---oOo---

www.ingramcontent.com/pod-product-compliance
Lightning Source LLC
Chambersburg PA
CBHW050530280326
41933CB00011B/1535